Non-formal Education

Non-formal Education

H.D. Kamat
A. David

CRESCENT
PUBLISHING CORPORATION

Non-formal Education

First Published : **2017**

ISBN 81-8342-037-0

Published by :

CRESCENT PUBLISHING CORPORATION
4831/24, Prahlad Street,
Ansari Road, Darya Ganj,
New Delhi - 110002
Ph. : 23272541, 23257835
Fax : 91- 011- 23257835
e-mail : campusbooks@hotmail.com

Typesetting by :

Arjun Computers
Delhi - 110051

Printed at :
Roshan Offset Printers
Delhi

PREFACE

Non-formal education means any organised educational activity outside the established formal system—whether operating separately or as an important feature of some broader activity—that is intended to serve identifiable learning clienteles and learning objectives. Non-formal education became part of the international discourse on education policy in the late 1960s and early 1970s. It can be seen as related to the concepts of recurrent and lifelong learning. Adult and non-formal education are essential not only for eradication of illiteracy and universalisation of elementary education, but also for making life-long education a way of life and for bringing about the cultural revolution for the learning society. These alternatives are inter-related and inter-dependent and both should, therefore, go hand in hand for achieving the laudable objectives. Since a lot of changes have taken place in the national scenario of Adult and Non-Formal Education, it is really essential to deal the subject extensively to give a comprehensive review and growth of adult education in India including the latest trends and issues. Literacy, critical factor for the knowledge are discussed along with emerging need, importance and challenges of the information/knowledge revolution in our country.

Schooling for adults who have never been to school or whose schooling has been exeedingly limited also tends to be labelled "non-formal". In many countries, during last two decades governments have established departments of non-formal education as part of their education ministries and have given them responsibility for all out of school education along with the responsibility of co-ordinating with non-education carried out by other ministries such as agriculture, health, rural development. Non-formal education occupies middle space between traditional school system and formal learning practices. The country has a very high level of illiteracy although its constitution recognises basic education as a fundamental right and the universal primary education as a basic state policy. But it is not possible to bring all sections of the people under the formal education system. A large number of children cannot enter the formal education system due to various reasons. A substantial number of dropouts also cannot get back to school. A non-formal basic education programme is necessary to address their needs. Imparting non-formal education at hours suitable for them is therefore, the only practical way of making them functionally literate.

H.D. Kamat
A. David

CONTENTS

1

The Boy's School

The school hours were fixed to suit the ordinary employment periods of the pupils. The morning session commences at 8.30 and closes at 12.15, while the afternoon period is from 1.45 to 5.30. There is a short opening ceremony for prayer and notices, etc.

CURRICULUM

The choice of subjects for the curriculum did not present any great difficulty. The limited time of attendance meant that only three or four subjects could be taken in addition to physical training. The temporary nature of the premises and the absence of workshop accommodation immediately excluded practical subjects. (This want has since been supplied.) As the type of education was to be as liberal as possible, English and Mathematics were made the basis of the instruction, and a four-year course planned. In the first two years the subjects taken were English, Mathematics, and Geography, whilst in the last two years History was substituted for Geography and Practical Geometry included in the Mathematics syllabus. Experience has shown that a rigid syllabus in the various subjects cannot be adhered to owing to the marked difference in the mental capabilities of the different classes. An example will make this clear. At the present time we have seven third-year classes with twenty to twenty-four boys in each class. The top class can do excellent work in English, History, and Mathematics, but they are far removed from the lowest class of the same year. The syllabus, therefore, has to be adapted according to the capability of the various grades, and to be made more and more practical in the descending order of the classes. In this connection it may be mentioned that students who have little mathematical ability have been found to do excellent work in practical geometry, and, what is more to the point, they take a keen interest in the work.

In Mathematics the work taken includes arithmetic, algebra, theoretical and practical geometry, the examples chosen being of as practical a nature as possible. In the teaching of this subject there is not the time, nor is it advisable, to follow the methods of the usual type of text-book on the subject, and it must be borne in mind that the object in view is not to prepare for examinations but to stimulate the interest of the student and to develop his mental faculties in the direction of clear and logical reasoning power.

The instruction in English has been arranged in order to teach the students to appreciate English literature, to read good books, and to write and converse well in their native tongue. Works by standard authors, including prose, poetry, and the drama, are read and studied, discussion on the characters and subject-matter being encouraged as much as possible. A well-selected library is of great assistance, as it is a matter of some difficulty to draw young people away from the badly written and badly printed, sensational and cheap papers which flood the shops of our newsagents at the present time.

Recently we have been able to obtain sets of books which the boys of a class are allowed to take home and read. This has been of great advantage, as it means that three or four books can be read each term, and it also saves much time which previously had to be devoted to reading in class. The authors read include Shakespeare, Goldsmith, Sheridan, Scott, Dickens, Macaulay, Haggard, Deyle, etc.

The syllabus and methods of teaching geography have been arranged to suit the capabilities of the various classes. With the first-year boys a broad outline of world geography is taken on a scientific and regional basis: with the second-year classes the Continent of Europe is studied in more detail. In the weaker classes the work is made more and more of a practical nature, and with very weak students the syllabus is based on the geography and history of the district in which the school is situated.

History is taught from the industrial and civic stand-points, and is particularly applied to modern social life and its problems. This has been found to arouse great interest amongst the boys, to draw them into discussion, and in every way to make the lessons much more attractive without losing anything of their educative value.

Physical training is a valuable feature in the curriculum and is under the direction of highly qualified instructors. The boys always change completely, under supervision, for the lesson, thus giving an opportunity of noticing the cleanliness of the body, and of taking steps to remedy any defects in this matter which may be observed.

VOLUNTARY CLASSES

In April 1917 the boys were offered the opportunity of attending school for a further period per week on the condition that they were prepared to sacrifice their wages for this time. About 30 per cent of the students availed themselves of this offer and a more liberal choice of subjects was devised in order to arouse interest. It was found possible to arrange classes in Art Metalwork, Elementary Practical Science and French. As this experiment proved such a decided success it has been continued and classes in Elementary Economics, Elementary Engineering subjects and Art have been added. The practical subjects have proved to be a great attraction, particularly the Art Metalwork, in which the boys with little intellectual ability have exhibited considerable artistic skill. A somewhat singular feature of this scheme has been the manner in which boys who selected French as one of their subjects have continued the class, very few having evinced a desire to withdraw.

One of the results of this additional period is that it has been possible to form a Matriculation Class at the request of boys who wished to prepare for this examination. Successes have been obtained in both the Matriculation and Intermediate Science examinations, and one of our boys is now at the Birmingham University taking the course for a degree in science.

DISCIPLINE

This question is one that will no doubt be of great importance when Day Continuation Schools become general, and it is quite possible that it may act as a deterrent in attracting teachers to these schools. It may be emphasised that there seem to be no methods of punishment such as obtain in fulltime primary or secondary schools. The maintenance of discipline will, therefore, depend on two factors, viz., the choice of suitable teachers and the co-operation between the employer and the school staff. Of these the first is infinitely the more important. The teacher must have a thorough knowledge of his subject, be able to illustrate it as practically as possible, and he must be prepared to work at the highest pressure. Discipline must be maintained by interest and personality rather than by severity, the latter leading only to unrest. A quiet talk with an unruly boy will generally lead to far better results than any amount of censure.

The co-operation of the employer and the school staff is very important, and has been found to be of great service in this school. The giving of rewards and the making of wage increases dependent to some extent on school progress both assist in modifying the attitude of boys towards attending the school.

Boys who have completed a three or four years course at the school are eligible for a certificate, which is given only to those who have shown marked progress during their attendance.

A few words on your experiences since the opening of the school may not be out of place. At first the boys resented having to attend and exhibited marked hostility towards the staff, no doubt because the majority had left the primary school one or two years previously under the impression that their school days were over. Naturally we had a hard and, what at first seemed, a hopeless task in front of us. After four years' perseverance and hard work the attitude of the boys has quite changed; hostility and resentment have vanished, and the school is obtaining a quite good tone. It has sometimes been necessary to suspend boys for very serious offences, but this happens only very occasionally.

As Day Continuation Schools are now springing up all over the country I wish to offer a few comments and suggestions with regard to their working.

First one may ask, 'What is the aim and the object of the continuation school?' and on this point there is an extremely sharp difference of opinion. On the one side we have the vocationist who states that the object of the school should be to train better workers in the various industries, and that the work of the school should be centred round the trade in which they are engaged. On the other side we have the non-vocationist, whose opinion is that the schools should exist for the purpose of training the young for their future responsibilities as citizens, to broaden their outlook on life, and to develop their intelligence in order to obtain a more enlightened democracy. The supporters of the former view believe that the boy is more approachable through his trade, and that discipline and interest will be more readily obtained in this way. This may be true in a few cases, but we have to remember that, in the future, industry will consist more and more of dull and monotonous repetition work on which the great majority of young workers will be employed. The curriculum of the school in such a case should not centre round the boy's work but should rather take him away form it and find him new interests in life. I quite appreciate the fact that there should be special courses for those employed in certain skilled trades, but even in these cases the general education should not be neglected: in fact it should still be placed in the foreground. A far more intelligent worker is obtained in the latter case and one who is of much more service to his employers. Again we have to remember that the boy's working time is only a small fraction of his life, and that he has more leisure time than working time. Surely, then, we must make provision so that he should be able to employ his leisure hours to the best advantage. The recent movement towards a shorter working week adds weight to this argument.

It is evident that, owing to the scarcity of material and the necessity for more houses, new buildings for the Day Continuation Schools will, as a rule, be out of the question. Use must therefore be made of any existing buildings which will more or less satisfactorily answer the purpose. This will be a tremendous disadvantage to the school and one that has hardly been considered. We have to remember that the boys have received their early education in somewhat palatial buildings fully provided with all those things necessary for the carrying on of the work. To come from schools of this description to others providing inadequate accommodation, and in which everything proclaims its temporary nature, at once gives the boys a bad impression, and one which it is very difficult to remove. I have been told again and again by the boys that it is the building more than anything else which they object to. In housing these schools there seems to be prevalent an idea that any sort of building will do, and I should therefore like to emphasise the fact that the buildings will play a very important part in the success of the school.

In addition to being the place around which the education of the young is concentrated, the schools should also be the centre of the social activities of the boys. This is of supreme importance. We have to remember that, under the Act, the staff will meet with the boys only on two occasions each week, and will therefore have limited opportunities of getting to know them. If the school is made a sort of open house every evening of the week, with all the necessary arrangements for indoor games and amusements, library, reading-room, classes, etc., opportunities will be created for the staff to know their pupils and to influence them accordingly.

It has been urged that such an arrangement would throw too much work on the staff. This will be quite true if the staffing of the schools is carried out in a niggardly manner, but with generous treatment there is no necessity at all to give too much work to the staff. I cannot lay too great stress on this aspect of the work. It is largely through the social side of the school that the boys must be won. This, of course, applies to outdoor social activities—football, cricket, etc.—as well. The physical training staff should be of great assistance in this branch of the school, and should be able to organise many schemes of a recreative nature which will appeal to the boys.

2

Problems of Class Teaching in a Boys' Day Continuation School

The management of a class in a Day Continuation School requires special consideration, since experience has shown that there are present certain difficulties which do not exist or are only found in a lesser degree in other types of schools.

Apart from the management of school subjects, which is really a matter for the individual teacher, there are certain general problems which affect all classes irrespective of the subject taught. These naturally divide themselves into two classes:

(1) Problems arising from external influences.

(2) Problems arising in the class itself.

PROBLEMS ARISING FROM EXTERNAL INFLUENCES

It is generally regarded as a truism that the success of a school depends largely upon the maintenance of an adequate and satisfactory system of discipline. This is undoubtedly true of a Day Continuation School, and it presents one of the chief problems facing this new system of eduction. Although Committees and Governors are partially justified in expecting a teacher to exert his own authority, it cannot be too clearly emphasised that in a continuation class external influences are often such as to render the most perfect disciplinarian powerless. The term 'discipline' is used here in its widest sense, not merely or even necessarily implying the maintenance of order, but rather the existence of a spirit of appreciation, industry, and attention on the part of each student.

To understand this problem of discipline the conditions under which the student comes to the class must be borne in mind. The student is more or less economically independent: the authority of his parents has begun to weaken: attendance is generally repugnant, and will probably continue to be so, until in the course of years the school has been able to build up a tradition and create an esprit de corps: ordinary sanctions for enforcing school discipline cannot be employed, and the teacher has therefore to depend entirely upon his own personality unsupported by disciplinary penalties. In such circumstances he may find his task hopeless if external influences are against him. A few examples will show this. Punctuality is a very large factor in the maintenance of any system of discipline, and will, of course, be enforced, but the attitude of an employer towards a school may make this very difficult and create a feeling of injustice in the mind of the students—a thing to be most carefully avoided. Inconvenient hours of work at the factory may render it very difficult for a student to be punctual; the boy in consequence feels himself harshly treated, and his attitude towards his school becomes one of hostility. Again, since the student only attends the class for a few hours a week, he naturally tends to regard his industrial work as of more importance, and he is often much influenced by the opinions of his employer and older fellow-workers. If through want of thought or, possibly, even through open hostility to the school, his employer or foreman prejudices his mind by disparaging remarks concerning his school, the teacher, will find him so indifferent or hostile as to render serious teaching impossible. Experience has proved how powerful an influence this is; really good classes becoming practically unmanageable owing to unfortunate remarks or incidents in factory or workshop. The same effect is often produced by innovations in the factory routine which, owing to the existence of the school, cause inconvenience or hardships to the students. For example, the alteration of the hour of paying wages may make it difficult for the students to obtain their money at a convenient time, with the consequence that the school falls into disfavour. These difficulties are not insurmountable, however, and will no doubt be happily provided for when it is realised that the interests of the employer and the teacher are identical; for although an employer or his representative may cause serious impediment to a teacher, the latter, if possessed of ability and strong personality, can be of great service or disservice to the former, by the nature of the influence he exerts over his pupils.

Akin to the state of mind in which a student attends the class is the condition of body. It is hardly reasonable to expect a boy, who has worked hard at manual labour from 6 A.M., or even only from 8 A.M., until 12.30, to attend school from 2 P.M. to 5.30 P.M., and to pay moderate attention to his instruction towards the end of the afternoon. Sleep will on some occasions actually claim its victims. Herein lies a problem which will require very serious consideration. Some favour attendance on two half-days a week for each student, but it may well be found wiser to eliminate altogether any industrial work on the day of attendance and substitute one whole day in place of the two halves.

From the teacher's point of view this problem can be briefly summarised thus. It is most important that the student should not be physically tired in any way, and, therefore, it is desirable that his day of attendance should be free from industrial work. This result can only be obtained by attendance on one whole day a week, for it would be unreasonable to expect employers to sanction two half-day holidays a week in addition to the two half-days spent at school. Unfortunately a whole day attendance has its dis-advantages in two respects. Firstly, in order to conform to the requirements of the Act of 1918, when it is in full force, students will have to attend for eight hours per week, and there can be little doubt that teachers will agree that eight hours' instruction in one day places too great a strain upon the student. Secondly, it is necessary that the teacher and the student should come in contact with one another as frequently as possible, but attendance on one day only would restrict the opportunity of meeting in class to once a week. It is not easy to suggest any definite solution of this problem, but in practice it is to be hoped that much may be done to obviate these difficulties by the existence of a spirit of good will between factory and school, which will produce accommodating arrangements of hours of work, whenever, possible.

Another difficulty arises owing to the changing needs of the factory, which may often appear to clash with the requirements of the school. The following is a case that may often occur. A boy attending on Monday is needed in the factory on that day. The head master is therefore requested to transfer him to a class on Tuesday. A few exceptional cases might be tolerated, but if such practice became recognised as legitimate, endless difficulties would confront the class-teacher. Transference unsettles a boy and breaks up the continuity of his work, for however carefully the classes are graded it has been found almost impossible to run two or three classes doing absolutely identical work at each weekly meeting. A boy who is transferred is therefore almost certain to find himself either behind or in front of the work of his new class, and this is apt to impress him with the idea that it really does not matter what work he does or how he does it, so long as he puts in time. Such an idea, of course, is certain to destroy the interest of a class.

PROBLEMS ARISING IN THE CLASS-ROOM

Even inside the class-room there are conditions opposed to progress over which the teacher has no direct control.

The first in importance is the building itself. Although the need for adequate accommodation is generally recognised by educationists, it is specially necessary at the present time to lay stress upon the subject. The demand for, and the greatly increased cost of, building material are so great that Education Authorities may almost be pardoned for ignoring or overlooking so important a principle. Moreover, the Committee appointed by the Board of Education for the purpose of considering this very question, in its Report seems to have been chiefly guided by the one idea of economy, and has in consequence published recommendations to Local Authorities suggesting accommodation in most cases totally inadequate. If this desire for economy at the expense of efficiency be persisted in the success of these new schools from the start will be problematical.

The class-room should be of adequate size, well heated and ventilated. Students coming from factories, especially in certain trades, are very sensitive to draughts and inadequate temperature. Moreover, the influence of environment is very powerful in a class-room of adolescents. A dull, sombre, and dispiriting surrounding, combined with bad ventilation or numbing cold and draughts, is certain to destroy the proper development of a student's desire for higher things. The natural corollary of this is that the room should be properly furnished and not overcrowded. Each student should enjoy the use of a separate desk, and, if possible, it should be so placed that there is sufficient space for a person to pass between it and adjacent desks on all sides. The practice which exists in some establishments (and actually recommended by the Committee of the Board of Education referred to above) of placing students in long rows across the room elbow to elbow is obviously very bad and seriously increases the difficulties of the teacher. Furthermore, the desks should be clamped to the floor or made incapable of easy movement, since students quite unintentionally often cause much noise and disturbance by drawing up their desks or pushing them into line. This is not so pronounced in an ordinary school, even when light desks are used; but in a continuation school, where, at first, folding desks may be installed in order to suit the circumstances of a temporary building, it is and will be a distinct minor evil, and the reason is obvious.

It is unreasonable to expect the influence of factory environment to disappear entirely immediately a boy enters the class-room, or that a boy accustomed to the rattle of machinery in a factory should be *lively* aware of the inconvenience of unnecessary noise in a class-room. This is an important consideration to be carefully borne in mind by the teacher. He will do well to realise this from the beginning, and endeavour to exercise patience and leniency in dealing with students who offend against school decorum by fidgeting, scraping of feet, and speaking loudly. To this advice might be added a suggestion that, since he will be dealing with a type of boy who is super-critical as far as the person of his teacher is concerned, he will find it wise to endeavour to control his own actions and attitude in strict accordance with the exhortations he addresses to his pupils, and especially avoid all sudden or rapid change of mood. In fact *he* might well take for his motto: 'Semper Idem'.

In the matter of teaching, each teacher will have to employ such methods as are best suited to the particular subject taught; and these he may only discover after much experience and experimenting, for the conditions will be abnormal. It is necessary, however, to arrive at some clear idea as to the general goal at which to aim, irrespective of the subject taught.

In preparing students for most examinations it is generally paramount to press into their heads a mass of rigid book knowledge, and undoubtedly the ordinary man in the street is only too apt to test the progress of a class by the amount of actual *facts* the students have *learnt* in the course of their study. It is hardly necessary to urge that the mere acquisition of academic knowledge is not the true aim of education, yet, since it is often the only *tangible* and *immediate* result a teacher can show for his labour, he is prone to exaggerate its importance and is encouraged to do so by the attitude of those to whom he is responsible. If, however, the mere acquisition of academic knowledge be made one of the primary aims of the new continuation schools—and recent evidence points to the fact that this is a real danger—disappointment will surely fall upon those who are anxious to promote them. It is fatal to attempt to impart knowledge in such schools by a rigid system of cut-and-dried class-teaching. The primary necessity is to create an atmosphere of inquiry and a spirit desiring higher culture; and it is safe to say that when a teacher has succeeded in doing this, and has also indicated the best lines of individual study, he has largely completed his work. The time is too short and the conditions are unfavourable to the practice of *intensive* education, even if it were desirable. The teacher should endeavour to follow the methods of *extensive* culture, and expert his labours to return to him a harvest *not* of exact detailed knowledge, but of the truer conceptions of life and a wider mental outlook.

In most cases it will probably be found impossible to give more than one hour a week to any particular subject, with the consequence that the teacher will best secure his object by dealing in a wide general way with his subject, so as to rouse the interest of his pupils and create in them a desire to gather the details for themselves. This is especially so in English literature.

To attempt to go closely through a book, carefully explaining all references and rigidly examining all peculiar constructions, idioms, and unusual words, is a method probably too advanced for juvenile students in any case, although frequently practised even with boys of twelve and thirteen years of age. To employ such a method in a continuation class, where the necessities of rigid examinations do not arise, is entirely mistaken, since it must inevitably destroy the 'human' interest aroused by the book. The aim rather should be to read the books of well-known authors as widely and as *naturally* as possible. If in the four years' course the students can be introduced to most of our leading writers—and it is important not to neglect our living authors—by actually reading in a general way some of their best books, and not merely being told things about them by the teacher in set lessons, they will learn to appreciate naturally what is good in literature, and will pick up unconsciously the rules of good style to assist them in writing respectable English.

Of course it is always wise not to push any method too far. The mere study of literature can never make a good writer unless opportunities are given for practice. There again it will be found best to allow the student to develop his own natural gifts by *self-expression* and, instead of set exercises in grammatical rules, etc., the production of essays or composition upon subjects arising out of the literature read will prove most efficient. In fact experience has proved that in all literary subjects, at any rate in a continuation class, it is advisable to restrict written exercises almost entirely to the student's own self-expression. Dictated notes in literature and history should, therefore, as far as possible, be abolished and their place taken by compositions of the students' own efforts, in which they endeavour to summarise at the end of the lesson what they have been taught or have read. Even this should be improved upon by occasionally directing the students to write compositions upon subjects of interest to themselves, which have not been dealt with at all in class, thus throwing the students upon their own resources for material. The teacher must not expect too much, or feel dissatisfied with his students' weak attempts. One of the most serious defects of our modern methods of teaching which becomes apparent in a continuation class, is their tendency to encourage mental laziness, since the student looks to the teacher to help him through his mental exercises. A boy will in preference do any amount of mechanical writing rather than *think* for a few minutes, but it is obvious that any exercise in which a student can escape by the assistance of his teacher, the employment of his brains, is of little value. This defect is even more serious in the case of boys employed in factories. Their industrial work is largely routine and lacks mental stimulus, and they are prone to treat their school work as if it were the same. The necessity, therefore, is to supply the stimulus, for although often possessing good memories, continuation school students are generally entirely destitute of the power of connected thought.

Finally, it is most important to encourage the students by emphasising the importance and value of the subjects they take. Boys earning their own livings are keen utilitarians and are *not* quick to realise the value of many of the subjects taught in schools, since their outlook on life is unfortunately too closely restricted to their immediate practical necessities. Until they can grasp the true objects of their studies and appreciate their opportunities, attendance will always appear to them as futile or even repugnant. There again, however, care must be taken *not* to overdo the thing. Students will frequently be found who are determined *not* to appreciate education, and will endeavour to excuse their insubordination by declaring that they do not see the use of this or that subject. Every attempt should be made to win them to a better state of mind, but no consideration should be shown to their plea. Any such excuse should be sternly suppressed or it will speedily run through the whole class. This is a problem which will perhaps only be found in a continuation school, but there it is likely to assume very serious proportions owing to the peculiar circumstances under which the students attend.

Class teaching in a continuation school is never easy. It is often sadly discouraging and generally exacting, but replete with interest and opportunities to an educational enthusiast who is given a fairly free hand. Committees controlling these new schools will have to allow a wide discretion to their teachers, and encourage experiments diverging far from the beaten track of orthodox methods.

3

Literature as Mental Culture

Language is more than the mere mechanism of thought. I dare almost say it is the thought itself, for indeed thought alone, if such exists, is but the embryo, whereas thought expressed is the child triumphantly brought to the birth. Abolish words, or word concepts, and then sit down to think! You can't! Besides it is our ability to speak that distinguishes us from the other creatures of the animal world; all God's creatures may think in a silent way, but to us our language alone seems perfect. But how many people are unable to use it! How inarticulate these boys are when they come to us! They spend many hours of their day in silence, in silent lethargy almost, and when they come to school for a few odd hours a week they are very willing indeed that we should talk to them, whilst they remain mentally asleep. Ask *them* to talk and it is another matter. But that is what we must teach them, and I have here set out to show that this teaching involves a severe mental culture for them; in learning to speak clearly and euphoniously, to weld together word and thought so that both become one, they are truly becoming educated; they receive an army training of the greatest value and become captains of much more than the words themselves; they are captains of the *souls* of the words. We have to teach them what to read, train their taste so that they pass by what is harmful and linger over what is good; we have to teach them, when they have found what is good, to share it with others; to read it aloud and make it live anew with the power of a cultured voice behind it; above all we have to teach them to *understand,* and oh, that need is great!

Only visit the law courts for an hour or two, find how many can *understand,* much less *answer* a plain question, and you'll sit in sackcloth and ashes, you teachers of England! Find out how many Englishmen can write a letter—straight to the point for business, and meandering round the point in that ideal friendly way which was so charming in our old letter writers. How many? Watch some people who plod diligently through every word of a newspaper, and end only with a very hazy notion of its contents; ask who can find all that matters in *part* of a paper, or read an article in but a few minutes and yet tell his neighbour clearly all about it. Listen to the bore who in telling a story takes you round the maze with him; or to the inarticulate person who can give you but a few sentences of information when you want fifty. Read in the paper how many people in Birmingham alone have been unable to fill in correctly an application for a ration book; or who have been unable to use the latter intelligently; and then ask yourself if the power to use language doesn't mean more than language—a trained mind, as well as tongue. How many know when silence is the best speech of all?

These boys, our future citizens, and leaders of their fellows, how can they move a crowd save by *talking* to them? The man who talks does more for the *living* world than the writer; and if he writes too he can bequeath much to posterity. The father who talks well bequeaths inestimable gifts to his children, who may inherit his gift, or who will at least hear and imitate unconsciously their father's speech. In clubs, in committees, these boys will have to speak to their fellows; they become councillors, guardians, and still they need to talk. Our highest council is the House of Speech (of Parliament) for how can man make his thought known save by the word? Perhaps, too, there is something akin in the doctrine of the Logos— 'And the Word was God,' the Divinity in man.

So much for the ideal. Now, how to attain? These boys, as I said before, are inarticulate, mute inglorious Miltons, and the one word embraces the other.

The first difficulty is that we cannot assume the mere mechanical ability to spell and write; yet it must pass without definite correction in the sense of mere spelling and writing lessons; neither can we in one short hour a week spare time to teach them formal grammar, nor should we if we had the time. It is only by free use of the language that they will gradually use it correctly. Surely if for foreign, highly inflected languages the direct method has passed muster, then with double assurance should it be used in teaching our mother tongue. Too long in the past England has wasted time in perfecting the part before imaging the whole. Children have been led through weary drudgery and have lived on the faith that the whole would come into view some day. In art, brush forms, however uninteresting, because they were neat, were the start; no little picture was allowed, because undoubtedly it would have been a daub, and would not have been good in the eyes of the inspector; in music, endless scales and exercises and no tunes; in French, only verbs; in English, only grammar; and these, too, often were all; the land of promise never was reached. But we have outgrown this in many things; why not in all? Why not follow Nature's method? Think of the fruit tree; how first it puts forth foliage, nothing but leaves, but then after pruning yields its fruit. Cannot the boy then make what seems to him a finished effort and finally have it pruned? The painter sketches all his pictures before he gives detail to any part, and I truly believe that the real musician, like Abt Vogler, 'fancies his fabric quite' ere he builds; then why should not the mere ordinary master of is mother tongue use it incorrectly at first, if you call it so, until some day he can complete the details of his building. I say let him talk; let him write; as much and as freely as he will, but let it not offend our eyes any more than one of those apparently useless sketches of Turner in the Tate Gallery; or any rough sketch of any artist. With boys such as these the mere formal procedure results in a cramping of their intelligence. They are wage-earners, some of them home-keepers; and they think on many problems; the thoughts of adolescence, the thoughts of youth, are long, long thoughts; and if they must only write or speak as much as they can write and speak correctly those thoughts must die for lack of expression. So I maintain that we must attempt much that seems too much; give them debates; let them discuss the problems of the day; let them read the newspaper and try to understand it, and to make one another understand it; let them write letters, draw up forms, fill in applications, make advertisements, write telegrams, sum up the meaning of a chapter read, talk about people they have met in books; let them express themselves. This is a harder task for the teacher than to give long interesting lessons. The boys need judicious guidance and yet the teacher must seem to stand aside—a very hard thing for a typical teacher to do. They must learn self-control; learn to organise their own class, their own debate; learn to discuss, to argue, to appreciate the highest things in literature, and especially to read to one another; it is only thus that they can learn the value of every word, that they will gradually discriminate between the stately diction of Macaulay and the racy freedom of Kipling, and know when to imitate each.

Some whose language is already fluent will need long 'pruning' exercises in the form of précis writing; others who are more or less inarticulate need training in the elaboration of a plain sentence, as so ably illustrated by Professor Adams in 'Exposition and Illustration in Teaching'; others, again, who have mechanical ability in the use of language, but whose power of understanding it is undeveloped, will need careful examples in paraphrase—oral for preference; and this individual training can only be given when the class is a small one.

Then, again, they need to find pleasure in the intrinsic value of words in poetry, and for this some work in verse deserves detailed attention in class. They need to learn how to read and enjoy a prose book; that can best be done at home; and in class, after, let them read portions of books to one another; let them talk of characters; dissect plots if you will; let them find what they enjoyed most.

But here are problems looming large, and threatening to efface our 'Châteaux en Espagne'. There will always be some who cannot, owing to home circumstances, and some who will not, read books at home. Again, these boys do not provide their own books and there will be some who do not faithfully return books lent to them. There will be many books needed in school if the literature is to be sufficient and varied, and where are the funds? There will be some who will sit silent through a debate, or discussion, and thus seem to be gaining little; there will be some who cannot do the extra written work that such a scheme involves; there will be times when a teacher, listening to the meandering thoughts, the faulty grammar, and ill-modulated voices, will wonder if it be worth while; if ever they will talk properly, write well, keep to the point and appreciate the best. But I have found that after all much is done and little is wasted, if half of them read books, and half of them debate and discuss, and some few write notes at home; then the work is not wasted, and if classes are sufficiently small all can have that training which they most need.

For instance, these boys are able to debate in a truly interested way on such subjects as strikes, for are they not themselves workers, men who may strike? They like to feel that they can take a side on an up-to-date question, or report on the day's news. They are interested in a Channel Tunnel, especially in its relation to the next war! They will talk on the subject of the foreigner in England after the War; on the costs of our Colonies; on Empire and Free Trade; on Labour Movements, and on the return of the Jews to Palestine; and they will talk eloquently, feelingly, if not correctly.

They will read a book, or books, such as 'David Copperfield,' 'Rob Roy,' 'Westward Ho!' 'Tale of Two·Cities,' and will have much to say about them—in their own way. They are willing to read selections, sorted out at home; willing to read little accounts of characters or plots, written at home; and glad to talk of current events.

Take, for example, a scheme of work for a term. Two or three novels are distributed for home reading; a long work in verse is read in class; short poems are occasionally read to the class; some compared in written work; two or three debates take place; a few examples of précis writing and paraphrase are attempted; the subject-matter is often taken from the newspaper, which is also used for reports. Then at the end of the term the class come prepared to talk about their books. A number of papers are written on say, 'A Tale of Two Cities'; and each involves thought on the work read, and ability to write these thoughts in coherent form. The state of France is told by Madame Defarge's knitting; Sydney Carton's wasted early life is shown in his last thought. 'It is a far, far better thing I do now than I have ever done.' The echoes of that little corner in Soho are shown as echoes of footsteps coming into the lives of Lucy and Darnay; Jerry Cruncher is the humour of the story; Mr. Lorry seems to be the thread holding the story together. Papers on such subjects as the above are read by the lads to each other, and this practical effort in thought and writing is not only valuable but enjoyable.

Thus though they come but a few short hours a week, and though perhaps but one of those hours can be spared for their

English, we have to try and give them all these—debate, précis, paraphrase, literature, reading; literary discussion; mere chatty calk of things of the day; examination of new words so surely creeping into our vocabulary; written composition, thoughts of their own on all sorts of subjects; and also the mere pleasure occasionally of having something good read to them by some one who really knows how to do it—all these, and in one hour each week, for three or four years. Some, we know, will gain very little indeed; some gain nothing; some gain very, very much. It is only then by the use of language, very bad use if you like, at first, that they will at last obtain that fineness of perception, that ability to go on educating themselves, which is, I believe, the highest mental culture.

> Tasks in hours of insight willed
> May be through hours of gloom fulfilled.
> Not till the hours of light return
> All we have built do we discern.

Matthew Arnold

4

The Teaching of Mathematics and Science in a Day Continuation School for Boys

MATHEMATICS

The place proper to mathematics in a boy's education no doubt varies greatly according to the ability and aims of the individual boy. In a continuation school with a four years' course the ability of the boy is the first consideration—the aims of the individual can be dealt with later.

Necessarily a boy's aptitude for mathematics will depend largely upon two factors:

(a) The training he has received in his previous school to develop his logical powers.

(b) The work upon which he is engaged.

Dealing with the first factor—By far the greater proportion of boys attending a Day Continuation School will have received nothing further in the way of mathematical education than is given in the elementary council schools, where, no matter what good promise a boy shows in mathematics, the teacher, owing to the large number of pupils he has, cannot devote any time to helping him to more advanced work. A boy who is weak in this subject is in even a worse position, for the teacher cannot give the time required for individual tuition that is necessary for helping lame dogs over stiles and almost inevitably gives some rule of thumb method—which completely detracts from the first essentials of mathematics, i.e. logical reasoning—or the boy is relegated to a lower class, where he may do the same work as he did in the previous year.

Considering the second factor—Boys who commence to earn their living usually take up work of one of three classes:

(1) Office work.

(2) Unskilled work.

(3) Work in engineering and other skilled occupations.

Boys who are doing the class of work mentioned in (1) and (3) will necessarily use mathematics to a greater or less extent in their work, but those in the second category will have no need for calculations as a general thing, and this class will give the greatest proportion of pupils for the continuation schools.

It seemed to me therefore, after I had been appointed to the Continuation School at Birmingham, that a scheme for mathematics must start with the knowledge a boy had when leaving the elementary school, and deal *generally* with the subject.

The pupils were divided into classes dependent upon their work. Incidentally I may mention that no class had more than twenty-five pupils, so that the individual attention which is so essential could be given.

After consultation with the head master—and for his many good hints I am under a deep obligation—I made out a syllabus so that—

(I) boys Engaged in Office Work should have a commercial course of Arithmetic and Mathematics for three years; in the fourth year they did not attend for this subject.

(II) Boys Engaged in Unskilled Work should have general Arithmetic for the first and second years and then Practical Mathematics and Practical Geometry.

(III) Pupils Engaged in Work of An Engineering Character, who were few in number, were catered for by having special classes in Mathematics for apprentices, the Bournville firm permitting them to come on two separate afternoons a week: the class they attended was either Mathematics applied to sheet-mental work or Mathematics applied to general engineering.

It has recently been found possible to subdivide the work of this section in accordance with the natural bent of the pupils. Thus we now have *(a)* Classes with an Engineering *bias,* in addition to classes taking the general school course with either Woodwork or Metalwork—conveniently referred to as *(b)* and *(c)*.

For the purpose of this chapter it is only necessary to deal here with *(a)*. In Mathematics the work is rather more advanced than would be attempted by a class in the same year taking the general course *(b)* or *(c)*; it is also correlated with the Applied Science as much as possible.

The teaching in Geometry follows the lines given below, but these classes very speedily reach a sufficiently high standard to admit of the introduction of Machine Drawing.

This subdivision has the great advantage that Class III (i.e. those boys engaged in engineering and allied trades) will in time become composed of pupils who have previously taken the course with an Engineering *bias,* and hence, when they become definitely apprenticed to a skilled trade, they will have a good knowledge of the necessary groundwork.

At the same time it must not be assumed that a course with an Engineering *bias* is in any sense a vocational training in Engineering.

The syllabuses are given in fair detail, but the reader must not suppose that every class in its own year worked completely through the course. Each syllabus was elastic and not rigid, so that, though the *best* class in each year was able to follow the suggested lines, the weaker classes were not: in consequence with the weaker sections more time had to be spent in dealing with certain parts of the work, and the treatment of various points had to be very much modified. Incidentally individual pupils, although in a weak class, were not infrequently below even that class standard—they had to be treated separately. To give an actual case—One pupil could not find the area of the floor of a room having simple measurements, i.e. he could not multiply such numbers as 9 and 14 together: the result was that he was taught to draw lines 9 and 14 units long, and make a rectangle, then divide it into unit squares and so find the value of 9×14. After some practice in such work he was given some cubes of wood and with them he built up various rectangular solids, and then by counting the cubes found the volumes, and incidentally learned that the volume generally for cube, square prism, and rectangular prism was: length × breadth × height. This particular pupil was able eventually to manage fairly stiff questions in areas and volumes.

It is decidedly interesting to note that all the questions given in this chapter have been worked by the pupils during their course through the school, and it is the more so when one remembers that these pupils, in the majority of cases, have never done anything more difficult than ordinary arithmetic. Thus, although the continuation schools will get a number of weak students and a number of weak classes, yet the standard of growth of logical powers, as shown by the work possible in mathematics, will compare not unfavourably with that of many secondary schools, which possess the advantage of having the pupils for five or six days a week, while we can only expect them for one.

It must not be supposed that, because the detailed work is on the practical side, the training given was vocational.

The majority of pupils dealt with belonged to Class II, and the whole idea in the mathematical teaching was educational. At the same time it must be remembered that pupils earning their living do not desire a truly theoretical teaching: the work they do must be shown to have some bearing upon practical things, which they either use, see, or read about. Otherwise there is no interest, and that means a difficulty with regard to discipline as well as great reduction in the value accruing to the pupils themselves.

(I) The syllabus for the commercial work was: Ratio and Proportion; Proportional Parts and Partnership; Percentage; Profit and Loss; Alligation; Chain Rule; Exchange; Approximation; Contracted Methods of Multiplication and Division; Logarithms; Graphs; Interest—simple and compound; Third, Tenth and Tenth Rule; Discount and Equation of Payments; Stocks; Metric System; Progressions and Series; Annuities; Problems treating of questions on Progress and Rest, Trains, etc. Certain parts of elementary Physics, e.g. Specific Gravity and Temperature, were also given to quicken the imagination besides developing the logical methods of stating in writing the various data given. Exception may be taken to placing the Metric System so far down in the syllabus, but this was done for two reasons:

(a) It was found that most boys had a fair working knowledge of the elementary metric methods of measuring.

(b) While holding strong views on the necessity for the adoption of the decimal systems of money, weight and measure, because of the obvious advantages: (1) the facility of computation which not only benefits the bankers and merchants, but above all others, the poor people in their purchase of goods in the retail market; (2) the advantage of being able to compete in foreign trade, using the same weights and measures as the rest of the world—yet since such a system has not been adopted by this country, I did not think it advisable to give undue prominence to it.

(II) The work done in practical arithmetic by boys in unskilled occupations during the first and second years depended very largely upon the class. It was found that most of them fought shy of a simple multiplication or division question in decimals, hence the metric system was dealt with in an elementary manner first, and at the same time simple questions involving the drawing and measuring of lines correct to $\frac{1}{10}$ inch or centimetre were dealt with: within a week or so the estimation by the eye of $\frac{1}{10}$ of $\frac{1}{10}$ inch or centimetre was considered, giving the pupil an understanding of the second place of decimals. At the same time it was deduced that the limit of accuracy was determinate upon *(a)* the boy, because of personal error: *(b)* the rule, because of its mechanical defects. Once having established the value of tenths and hundredths to a boy in this way, it was not difficult to go further and show that the decimal system was simply an extension of our usual way of writing numbers down, thus:

784-96	7 is placed in such a position that it indicates 7 hundreds, similarly 8 stands for 8 tens or 80, 4 meaning 4 units: 9, 9-tenths and 6, 6-hundredths.

Simple addition and subtraction of decimals followed, practical questions being obtained by drawing lines of definite length in inches and centimetres, and adding or subtracting, the answers being checked by arithmetical work. With subtraction it was found better to use the 'shop' method.

$$\begin{array}{r} 92.74 \\ 49.36 \\ \hline 43.38 \end{array} \qquad \text{Say } \frac{6}{100} \text{ and } \frac{8}{100} \text{ are } \frac{14}{100}$$

$$\frac{3}{10} \text{ '' } \quad \frac{3}{10} \text{ '' } \quad \frac{6}{10}$$

9 units and 3 units are 12 units

4 tens and 4 tens are 8 tens.

Multiplication involving decimals followed; this was at first treated by taking rectangles and in reality finding the areas thus:

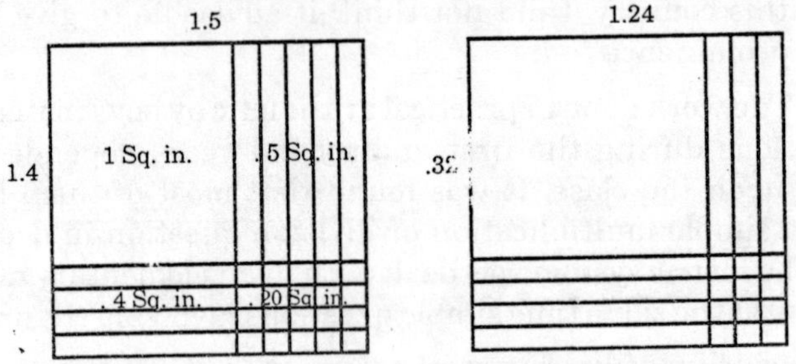

By simple drawing to scale, which the pupils were soon able to do, it was quite easy to work to 100ths in the lines; following this method it was not difficult for the pupils to see why $.5 \times .5 = .25$, etc. Powers of the second order thus could be introduced; at the same time it was insisted upon that a rough or approximate answer must *first* be obtained, so that it could be clearly seen—by the pupil himself that 71.84×6.72 must be of the order of 400 and *not* of 4000. It followed from the above diagrammatic methods that units × tenths gave tenths, etc., so that there was no difficulty about fixing the decimal point of the product.

Division followed as the converse of multiplication, and if a rough answer were insisted upon, there was no difficulty as regards the final answer—square root naturally followed.

Questions on elementary mensuration were next dealt with—areas first, sheets of metal of various sorts being used and measurements made by the pupils, themselves; then volumes dealing with actual models of wood and metal and finally weights.

Specific gravity was not introduced as such, but was brought in as 1 cubic inch of iron weighs .26 Ib., etc.

Simple fractions were then taken: in many cases it really amounted to revision. Time, however, was not devoted to complicated fractions, the most difficult being the simplification of, say:

$$\frac{\frac{2}{3}-\frac{1}{7}\text{ of }3\frac{1}{2}}{\frac{3}{5}\text{ of }3\frac{1}{3}-\frac{1}{4}}$$

Questions involving ratio and proportion followed, then variation, stress being laid upon practical questions.

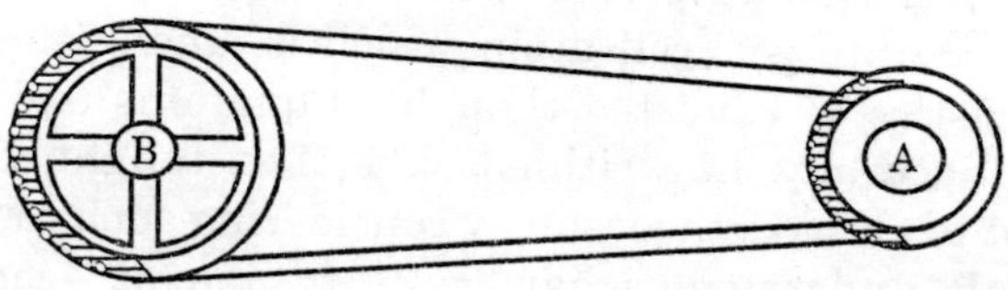

Diagram shows the toothed wheels of a cycle, connected by the chain.

$$\text{Then } \frac{\text{Number of revolutions of A}}{\text{Number of revolutions of B}} = \text{Velocity ratio.}$$

$$\text{i.e. } \frac{\text{Number of teeth on B}}{\text{Number of teeth on A}} = \text{Velocity ratio.}$$

This question introduced the pupil to finding the 'gear of a cycle,' the working of a 'three-speed gear,' and the value of a 'chain drive'—all points of interest to the average boy. Many boys, apparently totally unmathematical, could explain that the use of chain-driving eliminated 'slip' and that efficiency was high: that chain drives occupy little space and give efficient service at centre distances too short for belts and too long for gearing.

Similarly with regard to variation: the pupils have found from previous work that the volume of a rectangular prism depends upon its length, breadth and height—he has really done it by considering unit cubes: he now sees that $V \alpha h$, $V \alpha l$, $V \alpha b$. Whenever possible this was further brought out by elementary graphs. Miscellaneous problems dealing with train questions, currents, etc., were next introduced, and finally such questions as involved Partnership, Profit and Loss, Percentage, and Simple Interest.

In the third and fourth years the mathematical teaching consisted of Practical Mathematics and Geometry.

Consider first the Practical Mathematics done by the unskilled boy. More advanced work in mensuration than had been dealt with in the two previous years was first taken. This involved (1) more frequent use of approximate answers as a preliminary to the obtaining of the 'exact' answer at this stage, therefore contracted methods of multiplication and division were introduced; (2) the more frequent use of letters to stand for quantities, whose values were known or required—thus bringing out the accurate generalisation which is among the essential characteristics of educated thought. Equations and problems followed naturally. Logarithms were then taught, care being taken not to obscure the issue by considering such cases as 'a".' The pupils understood what 2^2, 3^3, 5^2, meant—each having significance from their mensuration work: in consequence this was the starting point. Logarithms were then defined and the utility of the base shown. It was quite clear to the pupils that

$$10^1 \times 10^2 = 10 \times 100 = 1000\text{: was also } 10^{1+2} = 10^3.$$

$$\text{Similarly } \frac{10^3}{10^1} = \frac{1000}{10} = 100\text{: was also } 10^{3-1} = 10^2.$$

Dealing with numbers not exact powers of 10, the following method was adopted.

78.43 was greater than 10, but less than 100—hence its logarithm was greater than 1 but less than 2. It was found convenient to work at first from the standpoint that such a number was 7.843 × 10, hence the logarithm was the logarithm 7.843 + log 10; the log 7.843 was obtained from the tables and then log 10, i.e. 1, prefixed—this method of 'standard form' was easily adaptable for any number, e.g. .0847 = 8.47÷100—hence log .0847 = log 8.47—log 100, which brings in the negative characteristic. The tables of 'antilogarithms' were used to reverse the process, but it was first shown by examples that the tables of logs could be used both for:

(1) Finding the log of a number.

(2) Finding a number of which one knew the logarithm.

Problems on mensuration—logarithms being used–were then taken, and also such questions of evaluation and formulae as:

$$\text{H.P. of steam engine} = \frac{\text{PLAN}}{33000}$$

$$\text{H.P. of turbine} = \frac{\frac{W}{64}(V_1^2 - V_2^2}{33000}$$

These questions caused the pupils to desire information on the relative value of a steam-engine and a steam-turbine—the second formula of course applies to a water-turbine—and in consequence the interest of the class was kept alive and the mathematics of the calculation was thus shown to have a very practical application.

The use of the slide rule was now taken and compound interest problems with harder questions on variation, etc., followed.

Graphs followed, up to the standard of finding the equation of a straight line or, to put it practically, to find the law which seems to connect two quantities one of which depends upon another, their various values being obtained by experiment. Here is an example: 'The following values were obtained in an experiment showing the head of water H in feet and the resulting pressure P in lbs. per sq. in.

H . .	1.13	2.24	3.37	4.53
P . .	0.49	0.96	1.45	1.97

Draw a graph showing the relation between H and P and find the law connecting H and P.'

A little work on Trigonometrical ratios completed the syllabus.

In commencing Practical Geometry with students of this type the first step was, necessarily, to get them to draw a *good* line of *definite* length, then to use a protractor, compasses, and set squares. Much of this work was most conveniently done by considering a line rotating about one end from its initial position.

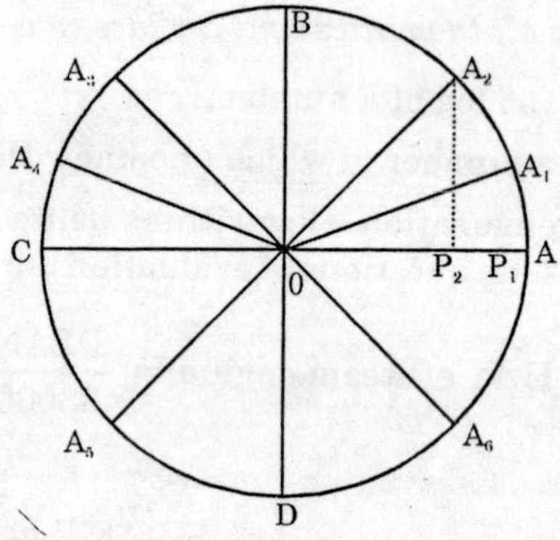

Its various positions are indicated by OA, OA_1, OB. etc. The line OA had to be drawn between two definite points O and A, a definite distance apart, say 1½ in. A position such as OA_1 was then drawn and the *amount* of rotation or angle was measured by means of a protractor: similarly for angles AOA_2 and A_2OB: these results were then added and tested by measuring angle AOB = 90° or 1 right angle, etc.

From this one diagram it was possible to deduce:

(1) A definite on an angle.

(2) A definition and value of a right angle.

(3) A definition and value of a straight angle.

(4) Value of complementary angles.

(5) Value of supplementary angles.

(6) The locus of A as it moves, always at the same distance from O, was the circumference of a circle with O as centre and OA as radius.

(7) If perpendiculars were drawn from A_1, A_2, etc., on to OA, and their lengths measured, then A_1P_1, A_2P_2 did not increase *to the same extent* or *in the same ratio* as the angle increased. With most of the classes this exercise was sufficient, but where not so, a similar diagram with some of the points of a mariner's compass was taken.

The syllabus then proceeded thus: Bisection of lines and angles, construction of lines at right angles to other lines and parallel to other lines; construction of simple figures, e.g.

equilateral, isosceles and scalene triangles, square, rectangle, parallelogram; proofs by measurements that (1) sum of angles of a triangle = 180°; (2) angles of an equilateral triangle are equal; (3) angles at base of isosceles triangle are equal; (3*a*) by deduction, external angles at base of isosceles triangle are equal; (4) area of parallelogram = base × height; (5) area of triangle = $\frac{\text{base} \times \text{height}}{2}$; and further work gave us areas of quadrilateral, trapezium, etc., while the use of parallels gave us a method of reduction of, say, a pentagon to a triangle of equivalent area.

Drawings were made of quadrilaterals and irregular polygons, with measurements of the angles of the figures, from which result the pupils deduced that the sum of angles of the figure + 4 right angles = twice as many right angles as the figure has sides. Hence we obtained a method of constructing a regular pentagon, hexagon, etc.;

$$\text{e.g. angle of regular pentagon} = \frac{2 \times 5 - 4\,\text{right angles}}{5}$$

$$= 1\frac{1}{5} = 108^\circ$$

Problems followed on the construction of triangles and quadrilaterals, given certain data. Simple scales were then taken and afterwards diagonal scales. At the same time the class considered similar triangles, the pupils themselves measuring the corresponding sides, and hence deducing the values of various lengths on a diagonal scale. Simple problems on scale drawing were then considered, and when possible actual problems of the height of a spire or the width of a road were obtained by the use of a simple theodolite. Field questions also came in, and the areas were obtained by measurement from the drawings to scale on squared paper, and by calculation.

Work on Pythagoras' Theorem and associated questions led up to the geometrical method of finding square roots; circles, their angular properties and tangency, were next dealt with; and then followed problems requiring constructions which necessitated a knowledge of the facts deduced.

Trigonometrical ratios were obtained by drawing right-angled triangles and the values of $\frac{\text{base}}{\text{hypotenuse}}$, etc., for several triangles with same angles obtained thus:—

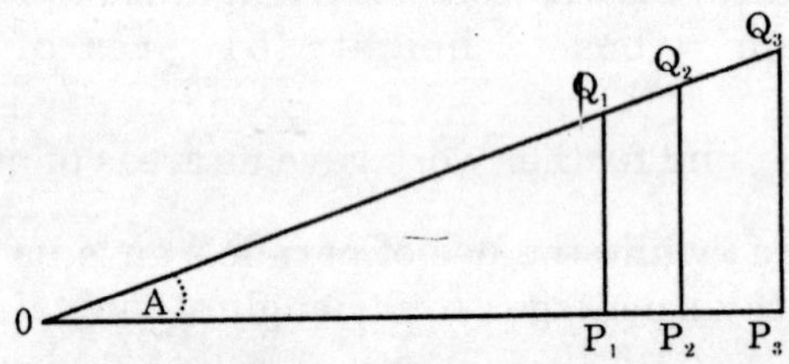

This work was correlated with the Practical Mathematics. If time permitted, we took more advanced work on loci, leading to the ellipse, and then plans and elevations of simple solids followed.

(III) The work for students apprenticed to skilled trades was both educational and vocational, the type of study depending upon whether the pupils were in the general engineering or sheet metal shops, but in either case the earlier part of the course comprised: approximations, logarithms, slide rule, and evaluation of formulæ.

After the first three years it was found possible to modify the syllabus of the first and second years in Mathematics so that more algebra was taken and less arithmetic. This was due, to a great extent, to the fact that we then obtained the pupils immediately on their leaving the elementary schools, so that there was no break in the continuity of teaching—hence not so much revision was required. The geometry work has also been added to, so that we now take plans and elevations of simple solids much earlier, and sections of solids made by planes can be introduced, also simple machine drawing. This gives us quite good work without detracting from the logical training of which mathematics is so capable.

I must not omit to mention that we now have one class—a voluntary one—which takes either art or practical metal work for half the time and geometric design for the remaining one and a half hours. This work, though only recently started, shows good promise, and much elementary deductive reasoning is obtained before the necessary constructions for design can be carried out.

SCIENCE

The Science teaching was greatly handicapped for the first two or three years by our having no room definitely set apart for such work. However, general elementary physics and mechanics were given, the pupils themselves performing the experiments wherever possible. In this work it was shown that it was useless to weigh correctly to 1 in 1000 unless all other quantities obtained experimentally could be determined to the same degree of accuracy.

In the first instance the classes taking science consisted of pupils who were below educational 'par' and who did not take the practical arithmetic, so that a considerable amount of the work was necessarily of a very elementary nature and the mathematics was taken in conjunction with the science.

The following work was attempted: Densities by means of s.g. bottle, flotation and hydrometers, together with discussion of forces, centre of gravity, etc. This involved graduated deductive reasoning and some calculations. Fluid pressure was approached not from the barometer but from pressure gauges which most pupils had seen used. Questions such as: 'What forces have to be considered before the necessary strength of the casing of a submarine can be determined?' or 'A hoarding is placed in an exposed position: what force or forces determine the strength of the uprights, etc.?' brought out pressure very well, and it was not difficult to arrange apparatus illustrating: (1) That pressure of water depended on depth; (2) That pressure of water depended on area considered. Then came work on the barometer and Boyle's Law.

A more exhaustive treatment of forces followed: parallelogram of forces, forces which produce rotation, etc., leading up to simple machines.

During the last two years or so we have been fortunate in obtaining the use of a room which has been fitted up as a laboratory, where work in Science can be carried out much more effectually than formerly, and we are now able to take Elementary Chemistry in addition to Physics. At frequent intervals the whole or part of the time devoted to Science has been given up to questions. The pupils have asked any questions they have cared to with regards to Science and its application to industry. This has been eminently successful, as it has caused the boys to notice things for themselves, so that they may bring their difficulties to the class meeting, and the result has been that very interesting discussions have taken place. Before very long I hope to extend this side of the Science teaching and devote a lesson time periodically say, once a month, to considering the making of models (e.g. steam-engine) and the difficulties encountered. This, of course, will be taken with the pupils attending Mechanics.

The recent subdivision towards a bias, mentioned previously, has made it possible for us to develop the Science side very considerably. In addition to the elementary work outlined we now aim at, and in the more advanced classes reach work dealing with: Stress, strain, strength of beams, riveted joints, mechanical advantage, friction, hydraulics, etc.

5

Physical Training in a Boys's Day Continuation School

Physical training is in 'the air'. Is it to stay there or is it to became part and parcel of the Continuation School? Are we to become a nation of 'good animals' or are we to gradually sink in the physical standard? If the former two things are required, first, the body must be given a fair chance of development by physical education, and second, the factory conditions must be drastically altered. Of the factory conditions I leave it for others to speak, but I cannot plead too hard for physical education to go hand in hand with the mental training of the coming schools. The army authorities discovered its great value in building up the human body as an efficient fighting machine. See the young recruit after a few months' training. The narrow chest and round shoulders give place to a breadth, depth and fullness; an alertness and self-reliance in place of the slouch, which make it seem almost impossible that we are observing the same person.

If we as a nation are to hold our own, then our men of the future must possess a highly developed, well-trained brain. But can such a brain be found in the undeveloped, unsound body? No; the body required to supply such a brain must be well built and vigorous—a body that will stand by its owner when severe indoor or outdoor work is required, when long hours have to be spent at the desk or in the workshop. Who is going to do the better brain work—he whose brain is steadily fed with healthy, rich blood made by the perfect machine, or he who, by the neglect of his muscular system, lacks the vigorous heart, lungs, and digestive system? Assuredly the former; for moderate muscular work will strengthen heart, longs and digestion, whereas neglect of the muscular system will cause them to become weak and trouble-some. Let us then be guided by the experience of the army and by judicious exercise give to the whole of our youth the opportunities now given to the few. Not with the idea of making efficient fighting machines, but for the purpose of creating such a race as shall have a joy in life arising from a strong, healthy, vigorous manhood and womanhood, that shall be able to laugh at the little worries that must come along, feeling me to be a glorious thing, a life founded on superb health, for health is the one thing most desirable in life.

The strong, healthy, well-set-up body will benefit its owner not only in the present but perhaps more so in the future, for it will lay up such a store of vitality and stamina that shall carry it ever onward through life to a ripe old age. Even if perfection is not reached, it is as well to remember that 'a bright and uncommon head on a broken down, or nearly broken down, body is not going to make half as effective a man in the life-race as a little duller head and a good deal better body.'

Life from a muscular point of view is becoming very easy. By the increased facility for travelling we are forgetting how to walk. Instead of weights being lifted by muscular effort a button is pressed and machinery performs the task which in the past had to be done by human effort. This is recognised by Henry Drummond, who, in 'The Ascent of Man,' says: 'So great indeed is the advantage of increased mechanical supplements to the physical frame rather than exercising the physical frame itself, that this will become nothing short of a temptation, and not the least anxious task of future civilisation will be to prevent degeneration beyond a legitimate point, and keep the body to its highest working level.' Let us by all means keep the body to its highest working level, and as a means towards this end physical education should receive its correct place in the curriculum of our schools. Looking at this subject from another point of view the question might well be asked,. 'Is physical training a help to mental training?' In games there is a spontaneous movement. These movements are not preceded by any conscious element; there is no psychological accompaniment beyond the muscular experience attending the carrying out of the movement. They may be called random movements. We give the minimum of attention when we do a thing from habit and when there is no distinct element of desire or purpose present. Hence habitual actions are often said to be performed instinctively, or automatically.

In physical training the movements are performed to words of command. In order to perform them the pupil must visualise as it were, and be able to detach the movement, making it a separate object. The command calls forth a response which has its origin in the brain. A brain activity is thus set up corresponding to the unfamiliarity or speed of the movement required. Take, for example, a quick movement where the command denotes that it must be performed at the highest speed. There is a quick activity in the brain cells, giving rise to a quick visualising and stimulating process by the performance of the movement, thus teaching the pupil to think and act quickly.

Mental work requires a sufficient blood flow through the brain. Exercise by increased circulation washes out impurities at the same time that it increases brain activity, and thus, if the exercise has not been too severed, there is a refreshing and stimulating process, leaving the brain structure in a better condition for mental work. Thus the break in school work for the gymnasium is not time wasted but time gained.

All voluntary actions commence as mental actions involving the use of certain parts of the brain, motor nerves, and muscles. Before an unfamiliar movement can be made there must be a concentration of the attention on the movement desired to be performed. This concentration varies with the kind of movement. Should it be a simple or familiar one the concentration required is small, but in the unfamiliar or complicated one—one requiring a large number of muscles to act at once and simultaneously (for instance, advance one leg, bend the other, bend the body forward, raise one arm sideways and the other upwards, doing it quickly to word of command)—it can easily be seen that a great concentration is necessary. Now what is the effect of this high degree of concentration on the pupil? Will it help in his study, in the workshop or office? Will it tend to make him into a more valuable workman?

Anything helping to cultivate the powers of concentration, whether it is through physical training, hand and eye training, or by means of quick observation, will undoubtedly help in quickening the intellect.

Physical training will prove useful to the discipline of our youths. When leaving school the boy has arrived at that age when he thinks all discipline should be cast aside. This is a time when he needs a firm hand—when the habit should be ingrained into him that he must learn to obey commands. The gymnasium here has a decided advantage. I do not mean that there should be a cast-iron discipline, but such as will cause the whole attention to be concentrated on the lesson, and in a subconscious manner the discipline here engendered will reflect and make itself felt in the life of the pupil.

What time should be devoted to the subject? At least one hour per week. This would give a lesson of forty-five minutes with fifteen minutes for changing from ordinary clothes into gymnastic costume and back again, for if the maximum benefit is to be derived the clothing must be such as will allow perfect freedom of the limbs. The size of the class should not exceed twenty-five. This number would allow some degree of individual attention. Experience teaches that if the lesson is given in the afternoon, when the vitality is low, it is not advisable to always conform to the routine lesson, but to give as much variety as possible, to appeal more to the imagination than the intellect. More relaxation should be allowed in the discipline and an element of fun frequently introduced. In the summer, if it is at all possible, take the class into the open and teach sports.

The lessons must be given by a master of his subject: they must be given by an expert, and that expert should be allowed to teach the system which he can make most interesting, the most alive to his pupils, and not be cramped and confined to a special system. Lectures should also be given on the objects and benefits of the lessons. The pupil should know what the teacher is aiming at. Get him to take an interest in the development of his body.

For compulsory classes music would not be advantageous, but in case voluntary classes are conducted in connection with the school, by all means have music. I gives a stimulus to the class. The pupils will not come for the educational benefits but for real enjoyment, and if music is a means of attraction, why not have it?

Competitive games will be found very useful. Divide the class into equal teams and appoint a leader or captain for each team. Give games of a competitive nature, by means of which points can be obtained. The teams should know the marks scored during each lesson, with the final results at the end of the term. Boys enter keenly into this class of game. The teacher should insist that the leaders take full control of their teams. They will, of course, be the smartest boys. Commencing their leadership in a small way will help them eventually to become real leaders of men.

One of the results of physical training is a decided increase in lung capacity. In the classes held at the Burnville Works the average increase is 25 per cent for the first six months. Now the value of a good lung capacity means considerable reserve for physical exertions and to meet untoward conditions, such as bad ventilation and diseases or many sorts. There is a still greater value in the fact that the extra supply of air to the lungs means a richer supply of blood and a decreased tendency to consumption. Big-chested people who know how to use their lungs are, as a rule, strong people. The child with feeble lungs, the prospective consumptive patient if you like, taken early in hand, will gradually advance in every direction. The flat, narrow and hollow chest will depart and a full, deep and roomy one will take its place, and the weakly youth, with a tendency to lean the head forward and thus produce round shoulders and cramped chest, will give place to the youth with the well-knit body and erect carriage—a future man of wealth to the nation instead of a burden. The cost will repay itself in helping to give a 'Grade I' nation

Where the city of the healthiest fathers stand
Where the city of the best bodied mothers stand,
There the great city stands.

Walt Whitman

6

A Camp School for Boys

In the first place the Camp School is essentially a school, but it is conducted under camp conditions; the warp is camp, the woof is, school, and the fabric is a most delightful recreation both for body and mind.

The instruction is essentially practical, and although a syllabus is drafted out before the school begins, a very large amount of the best work is incidental and, shall I say, accidental. It is the incidental work that is so very valuable because it shows to the individual that instruction and wisdom can be accumulated at every turn. Valuable elementary work is done in geography (mathematical, astronomical, economic, geological), history, natural science, nature study, literature, and surveying in all its branches, and in every case it is done 'on the spot' as it were. When these studies are pursued under conditions which the camp life affords, and when the theories underlying them can be discussed at ease, in the welcome shade of a wood or seated round the cheerful blaze of a huge camp fire, the benefits are bound to be greater, and the desire to pursue these studies further when the camp is a thing of the past must be stronger than could otherwise be the case.

That the practical work done may not be regarded as merely pleasant experiment and interesting conversation, a certain amount of written work is done. Diaries are kept rigidly, and practical examples it he mathematical and surveying work are done, while sketches are made when helpful. Without this there would be a tendency for the work to be regarded too lightly and to become subordinate to the camp side. This is a danger to be guarded against.

It has been our practice to devote the morning session to two or three lessons in the neighbourhood of the camp, and to take an excursion in the afternoon or vice versa. This is varied once or twice in the week by taking a whole day excursion to some place of note where work of a valuable nature is done. Perhaps I can best tell the story of our camp school by giving two or three sketches of our life in the camp school, and I have chosen quite typical examples. The first is our Monday in camp at Rubery.

(I) Rubery is a village on the borders of the city of Birmingham, about nine miles from the city centre. It is situated in the Lickey Hills and has an elevation of about 700 feet above sea level. There are two permanent structures on the camp site, which is in a field belonging to the Chandwich estate. One of these structures is a kitchen fitted with a range and large boiler and the necessary pantry and cupboards. The other structure is merely a roof raised on iron pillars over a raised concrete floor. Here lessons can be conducted in wet weather, and meals are taken at all times.

The boys arrive by 10 A.M. and all is bustle. Tents are erected in the lower part of the field and the company divided itself into 'tents,' each of which is responsible for one day's fatigue duties. These consist of preparing food for the cook and washing up crockery. The first day's 'fatigue' gets rapidly to work and soon we sit down to an excellent cooked dinner whilst 'fatigue' waits on us. Dinner over, there is an hour's rest to prepare for the first serious business, and to allow 'fatigue' to get their dinner and wash up. Then the boys are marshalled and away we go on a walk to learn at first hand some of the secrets of earth structure. We set off down the road to the quarry, and here we walk round and examine the illustrations pointed out. We note:

(1) The nature and structure of quartzite and its relation to sandstone.

(2) The difference between clays and sandstone.

We accumulate a fine wood stack and build our camp-fire, and as the flames begin to crackle and roar we wheel the piano out of my tent and sit around with our Scottish Students' Song-Books. From the flag pole we have erected the big flag is hauled down, so that it 'may not catch cold,' and with an obliging visitor from a neighbouring house at the piano we settle down to a couple of hours' music. The solo is followed by the full-throated chorus, and old favourites are roared out till the last notes come quavering back in echoes from the impenetrable blackness of the wood on the opposite hill. The greatest favourites are songs with choruses. As a variation the masters sometimes tell stories or read short stories or extracts from well-known books, while occasionally we hold a debate. The free life of the fields and the good fellowship existing between staff and school make this much easier and more pleasant than may be supposed.

'Fatigue' has just brought our supper down the field to the camp-fire, and after a hymn and a selected passage read from the Bible we turn in. For a few minutes a confused murmuring rises from the camp till all the boys are in bed, and this gradually subsides till only one or two boys are left droning out a conversation. The camp-marshal snaps out an admonition, and as I sit over my reflections by the dying embers of the fire, the calm peacefulness of the night seems to saturate my imagination. I soon slip between the blankets, and the countless weird little noises of the night-folk in the field die away and I sleep soundly.

(II) That terrific din which nearly caused me to fall out of bed, is Jimmy Anderson sounding the reveillé on his bugle. You must jump, for the day has come. The great red sun has not yet peeped over the brow of that eastern hill, and below us in the hollow the mists of the morning hide the coppice like a gossamer veil. There is a distinct nip in the air this morning. Swallows skim along over the top of the dewy grass, and here and there a late rabbit scurries into the thicker. Shortly we are all lined up, and after Bible-reading the whole party, except the day's 'fatigue,' troops down to the ponds and soon we are splashing in the water. As we come back the sun is just showing over the hill, the shafts of light turn the dew-drops into myriads of jewels, and sounds of life arise all around from bush and brier. Have you even slept in an open field, or—not so bold—in a tent? Have you got up before the summer sun and bathed in the limpid water of a lake? If you have you will appreciate the appetites that await breakfast.

In due course the time for lessons draws near. Today one section will do some physiology and First Aid with one of my colleagues. A second section will take the chain and arrows and will survey the field, make accurate drawings of it, and find its measurements, with another colleague. The third section are to study the contour of the district from the survey map, the model made from the map and from the countryside itself. We shall notice at the same time the geological peculiarities of the district and calculate gradients, etc. Among the geological peculiarities is the bed of gravel resting on the bed of clay, and the consequent line of springs; there is also the great wind-gap through which the main road runs. Much can be said about each of these phenomena, and the story of their formation can be made extremely interesting and graphic. These things affect the contour of the country, and also the nature of the agriculture and water supply. I mention these facts because of the multitude of things that come within the range of our work. At the end of each hour these classes change about until each has had its full course. All this work is done in the open, and when black-board work is necessary the class sits in the shade of the trees.

After these lessons there is a welcome rest and then dinner follows. This is always a hot meal, well prepared by a good cook in the camp kitchen, and the capacity of the cooking utensils is tested to its extreme limits, for the outdoor life has worked wonders on the appetite. There is a compulsory rest of one hour after dinner, before we begin the excursion which takes place in the afternoon.

The excursion for today is to the Cofton Hackett reservoir, the source of water supply for some of the canals which constitute a feature of the Midlands. The walk is most pleasant as we wend our way through the paths of the Lickeys and down towards the Severn basin. There are several things to talk about as we go. We pass quarries where faulting is clearly shown; beds of Bunter Pebble—these pebbles the villagers believe grow, for as fast as they are removed the weather uncovers others—and an explanation of their origin is given. We take to the fields and are struck by the extent of the rabbit-warrens. The reservoir is soon reached and a lecture given in which the following points are made:

(1) Nature of canals: necessity of water supply for various reasons.

(2) Advantages and disadvantages of canals compared with other means of communication.

(3) The place of the feeder.

(4) The history of canal construction, development and decay.

The return journey is most pleasant and we reach camp to find tea ready. After tea the lads play football in the fields, in which goal-posts are set up. It seems incredible that these lads had spent the afternoon walking several miles, but they quickly recover from fatigue. We spend the evening in the usual manner, and although we do not feel tired we are very soon asleep.

(III) We are very early afoot this morning, for much has to be done before we set out for our whole day excursion to Worcester. Each of us has to carry his lunch, and this has to be prepared. It is another glorious day and breakfast is soon disposed of, and the camp ground put in good order. Before seven o'clock we are striding briskly down the great Briston road for Bromsgrove, where we take the motor 'bus for Worcester. The clear air of the morning sends the blood coursing through our veins, but by the time we reach Bromsgrove the warmth of the summer sun has begun to make itself felt. We have not long to wait, and soon we are bowling along life Worcestershire roads at a fine pace. We reach Worcester in good time and make first of all for the Commandery. The venerable proprietor does not spare himself when he finds so large and appreciative an audience. The story of the Worcester fight is vividly portrayed, and we see the actual battle-grounds and the sites of various incidents in that battle. To me and to the other masters present the visit to this old-world place and the story we heard are invaluable. The interest of the young fellow is held to the last word, and as we eat our lunch on the grassy banks of the Severn, I endeavour to put this incident of the Civil Wars into its proper place. Even as we sit in the welcome shade of the trees we are able to learn a lesson in river erosion and flood-plains from what we see before us, for wide and perfectly flat plains stretch away from the river on both sides, while the river runs rather rapidly between fairly steep banks. Alongside, marks on the walls indicate the flood-levels of great floods, and so we get an idea of the vast amount of water that falls during a storm or a period of wet weather.

Next we visit the Cathedral. I can only very briefly indicate the points of importance. They fall into two great groups—Historical and Architectural. Not only do we see King John's tomb and many historic relics within the Cathedral, but various parts of the edifice, the cloisters, chapter-house, crypt, etc., each and all form the subject of interesting talks on the life and customs of the time they indicate; especially is this true of the cloisters. Then, again, the very positions of Chester, Worcester and Gloucester illustrate the importance from Roman times of guarding the pontis, and each of these cities depends for its site on a river. Of course this point was illustrated by many other towns up and down the Welsh and Scottish borders.

Now we make our way a few yards to the Royal Porcelain Works, and note with care and pleasure the process of making this high-grade ware. The educational value of this visit is very great, for it is quite distinct from anything we have done today. This is a lesson in practical handicraft as well as highly technical work; each branch of the process is explained by our guide, and we are impressed with the great amount of skill necessary to produce the porcelain.

The notes of the gramophone were filling the camp and the lads were enjoying a sing-song. We were soon in bed and there was very little talking after 'lights out,' for we had to be afoot about 5 A.M. for another strenuous day.

During this tour avast amount of educational work was done; the following are the chief points:

Visits to Baddesley Clinton—a medieval manor; to Warwick, Stratford-on-Avon, the Edge Hills, at the battlefield of Edgehil, Henley-in-Arden, Preston Baggot, and Aston Cantlow.

Practical lessons in geology, practical mathematics, architecture, history, and many other things too numerous to mention, made up a very full week.

I am afraid that these few lines fail to give any idea of the large amount of live interest which is generated on these tours and excursions, but as a teacher of experience, both in school and out of it, I cannot affirm too strongly that the amount of work of great educational value done on excursions and in camp schools of this kind is very much greater than that which could be done in a school in the same subjects and in the same time. My sincerest wish is that the example set by Messrs. Cadbury Bros. will be taken up all over the country, and also be continued and developed by this firm in the future.

ADDENDA

Each week's camp school consists of about thirty boys' whose ages range from fourteen years to eighteen years. They are selected from all branches of the works for two main reasons. The first is that no section or department shall suffer by the withdrawal of a large number of its operatives at one time; and the second is that, by taking boys from all departments, the school escapes the danger of becoming sectional and tend to break down any idea of class distinction that may arise between different grades of employment at the works.

I found it difficult to 'place' most boys with respect to their particular occupation so thoroughly effective is this scheme, and it was only in odd cases that the clerk or tin-box soldering employee was easily noted—of course I do not refer to style of work done, but rather to the spirit shown in the camp. If we take one week as a type, I find:—

4 boys at 14 years of age
5 " 15 "
11 " 16 "
7 " 17 "
3 " 18 "

These boys represented eighteen different 'shops,' even when I count all branches of the office as one, and all branches of chocolate moulding as one. There were boys from the following departments:

Electrical, Printing, Analysts, Scale Repairing, Confectionery. Office (all branches), Basket Stores, Soldering, Mould Making, Biscuit Making, Machine Bag, Warehouse, various Moulding Departments, and so on.

There were boys who were apprenticed to skilled trades and others whose occupations were very largely unskilled, so that the range of intelligence was wide but did not always correspond to the occupation followed.

7

Arts and Crafts

The development of the artistic sense is an exceedingly valuable part of the education of young employees. Those concerned with mental development have realised that study and practice in the Arts and Crafts help to a remarkable degree in the cultivation of:

Observation.
Memory.
Visualisation (mind picturing or mental imaging).
Imagination (and invention).
Concentration of mind.
Self-expression.
Taste.

In the exercise of these powers and attainments accuracy of detail, carefulness, and thoroughness in execution will naturally follow. To pupil and employer aline the economic value of such trained abilities cannot be over-estimated. The cultivation of these powers does not by any means exhaust the value of training in the Arts and Crafts. To be able to make a clear and expressive sketch or working drawing is in itself a valuable asset.

The appreciation and love of nature—from a simple wild flower to a glorious expanse of land or seascape—will be awakened in some pupils, and strengthened in many, by a course of Art training; and the appreciation of beautiful objects—from a simple bowl to a splendid cathedral—will be considerably increased after some practice in the Arts and Crafts. Such appreciation of things beautiful has a very healthy and elevating influence, not only on the pupils but on those with whom they come in contact.

The young employee's education must be on very broad lines; a truly liberal culture. Therefore it is our aim to lead the pupils towards self-development in the fullest sense.

The practice and study of the Arts and Crafts as a means of mental development will not only be valuable in itself but will act and react on other studies and on the pupils' work and life in the direction of spiritual freedom and development. To the young adolescent, with his many awakening and unformed impulses, the disciplinary value of regular attendance at a class in either of these subjects, together wit the harmonising influence of environment and subject, will exercise a beneficial influence at a time when the right kind of influence is so great a necessity. Therefore it is the high privilege of the teacher concerned to help to carry out this training, to educate more than to instruct, and to help to remove obstacles that are in the way of real progress.

Interest must be maintained throughout the course as the time spent in the practice and study of either subject will be beneficial to the pupils in proportion to the interest taken. We must have *enthusiasm,* both on the side of the teacher and of the pupil, without which little can be accomplished, and the pupil's *personal effort* must be aimed at rather than showy results.

Development under such conditions of study must increase the good taste and judgment of the pupils, making them more intelligent; more valuable to the community, their employers and themselves; in short, better citizens Much of the good we look forward to in the future will, we believe, grow out of a better understanding of, and higher education in, the principles underlying the Arts and Crafts.

I would like to point out that the principles underlying the training in these classes are based upon many valuable suggestions of Mr. Catterson-Smith (the Director of Art Education for the City of Birmingham), to whose valuable guidance the city owes so much, particularly for his insistence on the very great importance of the cultivation of *Memory* and

Visualisation, and his excellent advice to learn to design *in the material.*

The classes are held in the Bournville School of Arts and Crafts, Ruskin Hall, situated in the centre of the Model Village, amidst ideal surroundings. This, together with the splendidly equipped rooms, cannot fail to exercise a refining influence on the minds of the pupils.

The time devoted to Drawing, etc., or Metalwork, is one and three-quarter, or one and a half, hours per week, during a session of about forty weeks.

8

Co-ordination of School and Works

Messrs. Morland & Impey, Ltd., have been sending their young people to the Boy's and Girls' Day Classes for Young Employees for the past six years. The firm is not a large one, engaging in all between 200 and 300 work-people, and its trade consists in the manufacture of Kalamazoo Loose Leaf Books, including a great deal of printing and paper work.

In the first term in 1914 about forty young people were sent, including twenty-six girls, whose ages varied form fourteen to sixteen years. These young employees were not selected, but this firm determined to begin with a definite rule making school attendance compulsory for all who were working for the firm, or who joined from time to time.

It is important to state that the members of this firm have always been careful in the selection of their workpeople, and consequently their young people are likely to be more alert than the average. The employees are engaged under a thought-out system in order that the right type of person shall be found for the particular job that is open. It is also a rule of this firm that no young people are engaged who have not attained the sixth standard at the age of fourteen years, and if possible a child is chosen who has passed the seventh standard. This has an important bearing on the continuation school work, as it is probable that a very mixed result would be obtained if children were sent from a factory which had observed no standard of education, and it is certain that the difficulties of the teachers in the day classes for the young employees would be very much increased by the introduction of a large number of scholars who had been sub-normal through the whole of their career in the elementary school.

The works of Morland & Impey, Ltd., are situated in the country at Northfield, some seven or eight miles from the centre of the city of Birmingham, and nearly all their young people are drawn from the district immediately surrounding Northfield. They therefore have the advantage of avoiding all children from the slum areas or from the congested districts of the city, and as Northfield is more or less suburban, the scholars of the elementary schools are not of the slow thinking type that are found so frequently in districts far removed from manufacturing centres.

It will therefore be seen that the class of children sent by this firm to the School for Young Employees is probably rather above the average of young people engaged for factory work, and their experience might therefore be considered as one not likely to be gained by manufacturers whose works are situated within a city and whose young employees must be drawn from all classes in order to meet the demand for labour.

The classes for boys and girls are quite separate. The former is at Cotteridge, about two and a half miles from Northfield, and the school for girls is held at Bournville, which is a mile further away. The distance is a disadvantage, as it is necessary for the young people to go by train, and more time is lost than would be the case if the school were in the parish of Northfield. The firm would not care to have the schools on their own premises, as they consider that a change of surroundings for the school work is wholesome, and likely to lead to more concentration.

A number of difficulties have presented themselves since the scheme was inaugurated, but these have gradually disappeared with one or two exceptions.

The first difficulty was the great dislike of the continuation classes on the part of the scholars, and this appeared as a serous menace to the school work. This firm does not limit the classes to manual workers; members of the office staff under the age of eighteen years also attend. During the first few years as much opposition was shown from those in the office as from those engaged in the various parts of the factory.

It is probable that the continuation school was disliked by the young people because they felt that their education was complete after attaining the seventh standard at the age of fourteen years, and further school was considered as an unnecessary discipline and altogether too childish for those who had begun to earn their own living. This is not unnatural, as school to the average child is not popular, and all scholars look forward to the time when the close discipline of the class-room can be changed for the greater independence of the office, factory, workshop or farm, and the children doubtless think that when they have left the Council school, they have put away childish things.

Another reason for the dislike of the continuation classes is that school work generally requires more concentration than the early stages of factory or office work. The class-room does not contain the early excitement of works life, neither is there as much interest for the average child.

The parents of the children have generally been very much in favour of the continued education, as they can realise the great importance and advantage of further study, many of them having suffered through lack of schooling in the earlier years of compulsory education.

The children from the firm's factory incur no financial loss in attending the day classes, as it is considered to be worktime and is paid accordingly. Train fares are paid, so the children are under no penalty through compulsory attendance, but they have always been obliged to pay the very small sessional fee of 2*s*. 6*d*. per annum, and to purchase the necessary books and equipment, which only entail a very small sum.

Morland & Impey, Ltd., have not found it easy to rearrange the young people's work without inconvenience, and it will prove a difficulty, in some cases worrying in the early stages, as all factory managers can realise. It is not easy to dispense with the services of all young people even for half a day per week, although the half-days may be split up from Monday to Friday, and it is possible that some slight increase of junior workers would be necessitated by a firm adopting continuation classes.

The firm has found the difficulties of absence lessen as their experience in dealing with the problem increased. By careful arrangement it became possible to liberate the young employees on the regular morning or afternoon. During the last stages of the War, when labour was very scarce and the demand for young people for all sorts of munition work was incessant, it was often extremely inconvenient to fit in the school times, but, with few exceptions, it was found possible to do so, right through the War, and the exceptions became so rare that the firm strengthened the rule insisting that no excuse could be taken for, the absence of children from their classes.

It has not been found desirable to move young people from one department to another in order to make up for absences at school, as the change has a disorganising effect on the worker, and the different discipline through coming under the authority of various foremen is harmful and distinctly against the factory career of juniors.

It is opinion of this firm that employers of labour would very soon discover that the apparent economy of changing the young people from one department to another would prove expensive in practice, as the same standard of work could not be maintained. It will be necessary to duplicate the staff in certain cases where a man or woman is depending on the assistance of a boy or girl in carrying through certain work, but it is possible to obtain great assistance from the continuation school authorities, who are willing to fall into any reasonable alteration of school hours that suits the employer.

It is unlikely that the conditions of 1916-17-18 will be repeated. If it was possible to carry on the classes through the War, it will be much less difficult for employers to arrange their work in normal times.

It has sometimes been suggested that the firm should offer prises to their young employees for good school work, but the company has declined this form of reward as it considers it would be unwise for young people to strive for a gift more than for mental development. When scholars have shown special ability, or have been highly commended for hard work and keen endeavour, the firms have, in some cases, shown their appreciation by a present of books, the selection of which is left to the scholar in question.

The subjects taken by the young employees are Arithmetic, English, Geography, Physical Training, etc. The curriculum does not contain any item of a technical character, neither are scholars developed along lines that apply to the particular factory work they are engaged upon during the rest of the week. The opinion is strongly held that much greater development is possible through the study of school subjects, rather than in a technical education applied to factory work, and the firm would not care to liberate its young people for technical work only.

The experience gained by Morland & Impey, Ltd., during the past six years invariably shows the great benefits brought about by the further education of their young people; the development in some cases has been very marked. There has not only been an increase of mental capacity, but a nimbleness of mind has been noted that can be traced directly to the day classes.

It will be a fallacy to suppose that brilliant scholars at the day continuation classes are also the best workers, although it usually happens that such is the case. Boys and girls who have developed into a 'student' type are sometimes absent-minded and unsatisfactory in the factory, and in these cases pains should be taken to find the right sort of work, and when this is found a very valuable worker will be made in the course of time.

Difficulty has also been frequently noted among the young people of fifteen and sixteen who are altering very rapidly through physical growth, and not only their school work but their factory work is affected adversely during this time.

This firm considers the position of all employees every six months, when records are gone through and wages revised; at this time the school reports are always taken as a part of the records affecting the prospects of young employees. It is possible, by means of the school reports, to eliminate children who are unfitted for various departments, and it is probable, as time goes on, and greater experience is gained by continuation schools, that employers of labour will be guided very largely by this means in proper departmental selection.

It has been proved beyond doubt that the change from the elementary school to factory life causes intense fatigue during the first few months, and the occasional reversion to school life must be refreshing to those who are beginning manual labour.

It would be useless to expect good results from night classes which are attended by children who have been working eight or nine hours and are not physically able to concentrate on mental work.

9

The Employer's Part in Continuation School Work

In the concluding paragraph of his Memorandum on the Staffing of Continuation Schools, Sir Amherst Selby-Bigge refers specially to experiments on a voluntary basis. The following sentence occurs:—

> 'The Board understand that many public spirited firms of employers are willing to co-operate in such experiments; and they trust that Local Education Authorities will do all in their power to foster and encourage this development, which will both make possible the early absorption of trained teachers as they become available and also afford excellent practising ground for those still in training.'

Experience gained in pioneer work of this kind is by no means confined to the question of staffing. On the contrary it ranges over every aspect of Day Continuation School work. Inquiries on this subject are of very frequent occurrence. They come from many classes of the community, including members and officials of educational bodies, employers (both large and small), teachers, welfare workers, officials of trade unions, and even from individual parents. The questions asked vary almost as widely. Here are a few of them:—

How do you arrange to reduce interruption of work to a minimum when boys and girls are at school?

Do you recommend one whole day, or two half-days, or several shorter periods per week?

Are the students paid for their school time and, if so, on what basis?

Who appoints the teachers—Firm or Local Education Authority?

Is any distinction made between skilled and unskilled workers?

What kind of reports or returns do you get from the schools?

What action—if any—can the firm take if a student is habitually absent, or unpunctual, or guilty of insubordination in school?

Does the firm recognise good work at school and reward it in any way?

Does it all pay? Is it worth doing? What do the parents think about it?

To consider these and similar points this chapter has been included, but it has been thought well-even at the risk of digressing—to touch first on the general attitude of employers, both in the past and the present, towards continued education, whether day or evening.

As regards the particular students whose work has been described in earlier chapters of this volume, two or three points may be made clear at once. In the first place, all employees within the age limits of the scheme, boys and girls alike, skilled, semi-skilled and unskilled, participate to nearly the same extent in the educational opportunities offered to them. There is a variation in the upper age limit, but this only affects a comparatively small minority.

The second point is that none of these students have a normal working week exceeding 44 hours, while in certain cases it is less.

In the third place, it has been found that the only satisfactory method of payment for time compulsorily spent at school is by a system based upon eitehr average rates, or normal time rates which vary with the age of the student.

One point further may be of interest. Since this scheme anticipated the 1918 Education Act by a good number of years, it could not be expected to follow precisely the lines subsequently laid down by that Act. It therefore at present differs from the requirements of the Act in several respects, exceeding these requirements as a rule, but falling slightly short in the number of hours per year. It was also decided that as from September 1919 the scheme should be brought more nearly into line with the Act in the matter of hours, whereas those features of it which already went a good deal beyond the Act should continue. For example, the Act, even when in full operation, appears to admit of a student leaving directly he reaches the age of eighteen, whatever time of the year this may be. This scheme, on the contrary, requires the student to complete the school year in which his eighteenth birthday occurs.

A. RETROSPECTIVE

In this section it is proposed to discuss some of the ways in which, during the past ten or fifteen years, employers in this country have assisted in the work of continuation and technical schools. This work has been mainly in the evenings: the employer's contribution towards the evolution of the Day Continuation School will be taken up later. Any consideration of this subject—however fragmentary and inadequate—should be concerned with things which have actually been done, rather than with those things which *ought* to be done, and about which so much is said from educational platforms.

It may be argued that as *evening* continuation schools will shortly become a 'back number' they require only a passing reference, but as a higher type owes something to the less perfect types from which it was evolved, so the Day Continuation School movement owes much to the merits as well as the faults of the old 'Night School'.

The limitations of the evening class are too well known to require elaboration here. Nevertheless, study undertaken after working hours has played a worthy part both in English and Scottish education. Several firms now requiring their junior employees to study in the daytime gained their early experience in enterprises of this kind through carrying out some scheme of systematic attendance in the evening. There was an element of truth in the reference to 'tried students, taught by tired teachers, and inspected by tired inspectors,' but, in the face of many discouragements, the 'tired student' frequently surprised his more fortunate competitor in the race for knowledge and—incidentally—for advancement. The expenditure of time, money and energy on evening classes has not, by any means, been entirely wasted, though Mr. Creasey in his 'Technical Education in Evening Schools' shows that, in the past, a good deal of it certainly yielded a very inadequate return, largely owing to lack of system, or of proper guidance from those in authority.

In the introduction to his book on 'Continuation Schools in England and elsewhere' Mr. (now Sir) Michael Sadler says:—

> 'In all these countries public attention is being turned to the problem of continuation schools. And everywhere the lines along which thought is moving point to three conclusions. First, there is need for further limitation of the hours of juvenile labour. Secondly, the law should place all employers, including Government Departments, manufacturers, commercial firms, retail tradesmen, and employers of young domestic servants, under statutory obligation to enable young persons of less than seventeen years of age who are in their employment to attend courses of technical and general instruction for four hours a week at times of day when the pupils are not too tired to profit by the teaching.'

These sentences were written in 1907, and ten years later neither of the conclusions mentioned had been translated into legislative action, so far as Britain is concerned. For 'seventeen years of age' read 'eighteen,' for 'four hours a week' read 'eight'—and we have one of the main provisions of the 1918 Education Acts for both England and Scotland.

Employers, however, had not been altogether idle. Without waiting for legislation on the subject, many progressive firms had launched educational schemes, varying widely in scope and magnitude, but all in greater or lesser degree displaying the initiative which the State and the local authorities had sometimes failed to show. Those employers were doing something constructive while others, who formed the vast majority, contented themselves with grumbling at the mental shortcomings of the boys and girls who worked for them and wondering 'what we pay education rates for'.

It is difficult to gauge accurately the extent of work done in this way, even in pre-war days, but the attempt has more than once been made. Mr. Sadler's volume, already quoted, devotes forty pages to a tabulated statement of the co-operation effected between schools and employers, the result of a very widespread inquiry addressed to the firms. About the same time, or rather earlier, the Association of Technical Institutions carried out an independent inquiry, on the same subject but addressed to the schools, and published the information in pamphlet form.

An examination of either of these returns suggests that most of the firms giving educational facilities differentiated very clearly between the apprentice—be he premiumed, indentured, or what not—and the ordinary boy or girl whose future lay in unskilled or semi-skilled work.

Evening class fees might be returned—under certain conditions—to students of the latter type, but the youth apprenticed to the same firm would be allowed to attend afternoon classes at the local Technical Institute. In passing it may be asked why apprentices' classes in mathematics and similar subjects have been held in the afternoon so much more frequently than in the morning—certainly not for educational reasons.

This preferential treatment of apprentices has brought into special prominence the educational methods of the larger engineering concerns, as being the firms most given to the employment of regular apprentices, and placed such firms by themselves in a class which is rather outside the province of this chapter.

Turning to the work of firms not primarily concerned with engineering we find some interesting points. It is a strange fact that in general welfare work for the benefit of employees, as well as the furtherance of education, quite a number of the most active firms have been those identified either with foodstuffs or with other simple domestic commodities.

At a conference on social work in factories, held a year or two before the outbreak of the war, it was curious to find that the bulk of the firms participating were connected with one or other of the following:—Soap, starch, blacklead, metal polish, tobacco, mustard, jam, biscuits, coca, chocolate, drugs, printing, publishing, or dyeing. The preponderance of ladies among the representatives at this conference suggested that the special needs of girl employees were duly recognised.

The same tendency still holds good. Recently an Association was formed of firms carrying on Educational Schemes for the benefit of their employees. Connected with the movement are several well-known firms in the engineering and allied trades, but a list of products very similar to the above represents the activities of the other companies taking part.

During the last ten years it has been the present writer's privilege to come into contact with many firms—large and small, progressive and otherwise—to whom had been brought home some measure of responsibility for the education of their boys and girls. In some cases the feeling of responsibility was more or less spontaneous—in a few cases, entirely so. In others it was induced by the persistent visits, or the urgent representations, of the Principal of the neighbouring Technical Institute, the Organiser of local Evening Schools, or some other official of the education authority.

Take an average case. As a first step most firms would agree to refund evening class fees to employees who complied with certain conditions as to regular attendance and satisfactory progress. After that probably the privilege of attending afternoon classes would be extended to a favoured section, generally apprentices. As these students went to school in the firm's time, sessional reports on work done were a natural sequel. If these reports were fully made use of they became one of the most useful links in the chain of co-operation. The question of 'Rewards and Incentives to Study' (which some educationists disrespectfully call 'bribes') is discussed later, but it may be noted here that the production of school reports at times of wages-revision may easily become a factor of the utmost importance. In quite a number of towns the authority controlling the Technical and Continuation Schools has by systematic effort been able to bring about a much greater measure of co-operation on the part of the employers in the district. The interest shown may take various forms in addition to those already mentioned.

The following are examples:—Publicity for educational advertisements, notices, posters or prospectuses; opportunities for personal propaganda work; gifts of books, apparatus and equipment to the schools; remission of overtime; permission to leave early on class nights or to come in later the following morning; special wage increments on receipt of satisfactory school reports; prizes or rewards in money, books or instruments; financial assistance towards tram fares or other incidental expenses; scholarships or other means of access to places of higher study for those who do best in the ordinary classes of the district; library facilities, and convenient rooms set apart for homework. Arrangements such as these, combined in every possible way, form the educational schemes or very many firms. The initiative may have come from the employer himself or from the education authority. Some firms will readily grant one concession and will firmly decline—for reasons of their own—others which appear quite as easy to make.

Of the various towns in which the employers have been induced generally to give the educational authorities substantial moral support, perhaps the most interesting example is furnished by Edinburgh. The Organiser of Continuation Classes to the Edinburgh School Board submits an annual report in which prominence is given to the co-operation of employers and the methods by which it is obtained. One cannot do better than quote a couple of paragraphs from the report dealing with the 1916-17 Session. After reference has been made to war-time restrictions placed upon ordinary advertising, the Organiser states:—

> 'The other methods for securing the active co-operation of employers, voluntary agencies, and private individuals were again pursued with the customary satisfactory results. The annual visitation of employers was begun on September 11, and concluded on October 3. Over 400 visits were made by the Organiser and 101 meetings of workpeople were addressed by Members of the Board.
>
> In spite of abnormal conditions and dislocation of working arrangements employers continue to take the keenest interests in this propaganda work, and to give freely facilities for holding the meetings in a suitable place and at a suitable time, inside the works, partly in the employer's time, and with a responsible representative of the firm present. In a considerable number of cases a record attendance was secured and great interest was shown in the alterations which the Board had made to suit the changed conditions of the times. Over 1300 pupils had their fees guaranteed—the number of individual guarantors being 100.'

In September 1918 the writer was privileged to attend one of these dinner-hour meetings—the 120th of the season—and came away feeling that if more towns followed Edinburgh's example there would be fewer complaints of the comparative failure of evening classes. Few towns—possible none—in either England or Scotland can equal Edinburgh's record in regard to the number of continuation school entries as compared with available adolescents living in the district, and this without recourse to compulsory powers.

So much for the part played by employers in evening school work: in the Day Continuation Schools of the future the employer will have infinitely greater opportunities of helpful and constructive co-operation. But let it not be forgotten that, even when all 'young persons' go to day classes, the evening school will still contribute to the programme many additional (voluntary) classes, some of them semi-recreative, for those under eighteen, while those over eighteen, who, in the eye of the 1918 Education Act, are no longer young, will be mainly dependent on evening classes for whatever studies they wish to pursue.

The evening school may still say 'Resurgam!'

B. THE CASE FOR THE UNSKILLED WORKER

Leaving for the moment the apprentice and his preferential treatment in the matter of day classes, we now consider the position of the ordinary boy or girl, engaged in one or other of the repetition jobs which make up so large a proportion of factory work.

Until quite recently few education authorities seemed to make any special arrangements for these young persons: their requirements were seldom discussed by bodies voicing expert educational opinion. In certain quarters it seemed to be held that every boy of intelligence ought to become apprenticed to some skilled occupation and that, if he desired it, he could easily do so. A visit to almost any modern factory ought to disprove this view. Further, it may be submitted that the more monotonous a boy's task, the more imperative the need for suitable education to develop those parts of his intellectual equipment on which his avocation makes such slight demands. Granted good wages with prospects of advancement, reasonable security of employment, short hours and satisfactory working conditions, with an education such that he can spend his leisure profitably, is there any ground for assuming that unskilled labour is either unpopular for undesirable? The experience of the writer, brought into contact with many hundreds of factory youths, all goes to show that unskilled repetition work is, on the average, rather popular than otherwise. Its *desirability* is another and more difficult question. It is important not to lose sight of the mentally numbing effect apparently inseparable from continued close association with automatic machinery, but the business of the continuation school should be to counterpart this. It is sometimes urged that the machine minder raises his efficiency to a maximum by becoming as automatic as his machine. Apart from the inhumanity of this view, it may be argued that anyone of undeveloped intelligence, placed in charge of intricate and expensive machinery, is likely to prove—even wen regarded from the lowest standpoint—an unprofitable servant. All this may seem to be rather a digression, but, even so, it is suggested by one of the chief themes of this book—namely, that much-neglected subject, the continued education of the unskilled and the semi-skilled.

What has been said of the boys is largely applicable to girls. Perhaps even less effort has been made in the past by education committees to really *educate* the girl employed in a factory. If she aspired to enter an office she found shorthand classes in abundance with, sometimes, the additional attraction of a little typewriting. If her tastes were domestic she may have joined a class in cookery, dressmaking, or millinery.

The question of monotonous work is dealt with in one of the Reports of the Committee on Adult Education. One of those who gave evidence before this Committee put forward an interesting point of view which the following quotation makes fairly clear:

> 'If work of a monotonous sort is excessive, it will dull the wits of elderly men unless the physical motion required becomes purely mechanical and the brain is trained to be active in another direction. . . It should be possible, if education is continued from the elementary school onward, to make monotonous occupation an educational advantage.'

C. ATTENDANCE AT CLASSES AS A CONDITION OF EMPLOYMENT

In 1906 the firm with which the writer is identified made it a condition of employment that all boy and girls connected with the factory should attend an approved evening school course until the close of the session in which their sixteenth birthday occurred; three years later the age limit was raised to seventeen and in 1910 it was further extended to eighteen—the final figure for all except apprentices, office employees, and a very limited number of others.

The Local Authority provided the classes; the firm instructed their employees to join, using all their influence to secure regular attendance, and rewarded the students in various ways for steady work, good conduct, and satisfactory progress. The co-operation was fairly complete and worked smoothly. About the same time, or even a few ears earlier, several large industrial concerns in other pars of the country had taken similar steps with varying degrees of success. Much has been written and said on both sides regarding this form of compulsory attendance. It has been called by various uncomplimentary names, such as 'Unpaid Overtime' and even 'Educational Conscription'. The latter term was used in he 'School World' some half a dozen years ago by a writer who apparently spoke from unfortunate personal experience. The controversy as between voluntary and compulsory service has, more recently, been worn threadbare in connection with much larger issues and need not be continued here, especially as evening classes now take a subordinate place. One point only should be emphasised, and it is this. Assuming here that other difficulties have been met and that conditions are generally favourable, time—or rather the lack of it—is the fatal weakness in any scheme of compulsory evening school attendance. The total possible hours of attendance during four years, on a two-nights-a-week basis, seldom exceed 400—little more than would be included in one term's work at most secondary schools. This figure, also assumes an approximately perfect attendance for 25 weeks or usually one hundred hours per session, while the average number of hours put in by evening class students throughout England is more like 50 per session.

In 1913 the step was taken at Bournville of substituting *Day*

Continuation Classes for the previous Evening School system and a new educational experiment commenced.

For the purpose of this chapter, at least, Day Continuation Schools are understood to be institutions in which the instruction is of a fairly general type; where provision is made for girls as well as boys, for semi-skilled and unskilled workers, as well as for those learning skilled trades or working in offices. Such schools will show essential differences—in aim as well as in method—from junior technical schools, trade schools, or day technical classes for apprentices. The methods of instruction and of internal organisation, while these may vary between wide limits, they have much in common with those found in secondary, or higher elementary, or central (upper standard) schools.

This chapter, however, has to deal with the employers side of the matter. Any Local Education Authority proposing to establish Day Continuation Schools, whether on a voluntary basis or backed by statutory powers, would encounter three main practical difficulties. These concern, respectively, the staff, the premises, and the employers of the potential students. The first and the second may be put aside for the moment. In the experiment which forms the main theme of this book the employers instigated the scheme themselves so that the third difficulty did not arise. It must not, however, be thought a simple matter to release about a thousand juniors every week so that they may attend school—even with favourable conditions and the most cordial support from the heads of the firm. In a later section it will be shown how some of the special departmental difficulties can be minimised, but, in the meantime, it may be suggested that the employer and the local authority changed places in this case, the former becoming for the moment the pioneer and the latter readily falling in with the new proposals.

We have had very little data on which to base any theory for the internal organisation or management of part-time day classes for the general worker, conducted on any sort of basis, whether it be voluntary, compulsory, or 'as a condition of employment'—really a form of local compulsion. The number of experiments made has been comparatively small; nor is it likely that any voluntary scheme would ever attain to more than a local or partial application. Without the stimulus of compulsory powers, public opinion is not quite ripe for any general development of this kind:

in fact public opinion is apt to be rather critical of the employer who requires attendance as a condition of employment, and even in some cases in suspect that his motives are not disinterested. So it happens that real experience of conducting Day Continuation Schools has only been gained in a very small number of places, but this little store of knowledge will have a greatly enhanced value now that a national scheme has reached the Statute Book.

In those cases where the thing has already been done, some one must have made a definite move—the education authority, the employer, the young employees themselves or their parents. The last two may be put on one side for the moment as being most unlikely to take any concentration in this direction: the education authority might plan the school and invite local firms to send the students: the firms might ask for the schools to be provided and notify their boys and girls to attend. Up to the present first steps may be taken much more easily, and have been taken more frequently, by the employer than by anyone else. If the large employer commences, neighbouring smaller firms may find less difficulty in joining and making their contribution of students—more especially if the school is being administered by the local authority and conducted as a public institution. Another argument is thus furnished against the school inside the factory for the exclusive use of those employed therein.

D. WORKS DAY CONTINUATION SCHOOL OR MUNICIPAL DAY CONTINUATION SCHOOL?

Several firms at present evolving educational schemes are asking themselves this question: 'Who shall conduct the day classes, the local authority for education or the firm?' The answers to this question vary curiously and are, in some cases, worth studying. One concern will run its boys' classes itself, but will allow the Education Authority to look after the girls' classes. A second firm will do exactly the opposite. Another would like a position of complete autonomy cut off from both rate aid and Board of Education, but the 1918 Act requires inspection by either the Board of Education or the Local Education Authority. A firm taking the third view—provided their educational ideals are sufficiently high—will have a magnificent opportunity of doing really pioneer work which ought to live, with the minimum of inspection or external interference. The additional cost involved to such a firm will be partly balanced by simplicity of arrangement and management. The school buildings will belong to the firm; the teachers will be their employees; the hours of opening and the dates of holidays can be conveniently adjusted to meet works arrangements; the educational scheme can be closely co-ordinated with other forms of social or welfare work; dislocation generally can be reduced to a minimum. It may also be argued that a continuation school in a works is a convenient corporate unit in which a civic spirit is readily cultivated.

'Now we advocate Education, not merely to make the man the better workman, but the workman the better man,' said Sir John Lubbock twenty years ago. If those responsible for such a 'Works School' have consciously or unconsciously, taken this as their motto, as is undoubtedly the case in some instances, this plan may work to the advantage of all concerned—but it is a big 'if'. Should the object of such classes, run by any individual firm, be summed up in the word' output,' then the whole idea is fundamentally wrong and the classes should not be recognised as Day Continuation Schools within the meaning of the Act. A compromise—or rather a combination—which has much to recommend it is that all continued education which is quite general in its character should be administered by the local authority, inspected and assisted by the State and aided, if necessary, from the education rates of the district. General education is, or ought to be, a marketable as well as a portable commodity, which the continuation school student may take with him from one employer to another. It is, in fact, a national rather than a personal asset. It is therefore reasonable to ask that it shall be provided from pubic funds. On the other hand, instruction in methods or processes practised only by one factory in the district may quite well be given within the factory by experts in the employment of the firm. In fact this is probably the best way of providing highly specialised instruction, but such teaching should be supplementary to the work of the general Day Continuation School, and should not, to any extent, replace it. Just as it is hardly the duty of the ratepayer to provide technical training which will benefit one employer almost exclusively, so it is not—or at least should not be—the employer's business to undertake educational work of a perfectly general kind, though some firms have found themselves compelled to do this. A division of responsibility on the lines here suggested is quite equitable and experience has shown that a Works Educational Scheme can be satisfactorily built up on such a twofold basis. (One criticism brought against this view is that general and vocational education can best be co-ordinated if they are undertaken by the same authority, but this argument hardly applies to any except skilled workers.)

There is also a further point of view. Change of environment from factory to school should prove beneficial, and intercourse with employees of another firm attending the same classes has its own educational value. Conversation, at the age in question, is largely a comparison of personal experiences and an interchange of views on daily work and daily grievances—half-formed views no doubt, and crudely expressed, but nonethe less sincere. It is all to the good, and makes for breadth of outlook, that students doing different kinds of work, under employers and foremen of varying calibre, should meet under common conditions (not only in the same day school, but in the corporate life of the school as well) and should be brought to realise that grievances are confined to no one factory. This is especially the case if such subjects as Citizenship, Industrial History, Factory Legislation, the Whitley Report, etc., are studied, and if the method of debate or discussion is employed in teaching them. Similar reasons might be given why all those who contemplate teaching in a particular town, for instance, should not be educated in one and the same training college.

As Day Continuation School Schemes are commenced in increasing numbers by various firms and groups of firms, it becomes evident that there will be no clear line of demarcation between Works Schools and the other variety. Co-operation and division of responsibility have already appeared in quite a variety of forms. For example, there are several cases where teachers supplied by the Education Authority carry on a school in a building provided by the firm—even, in some cases, inside the factory itself. There are also examples in which some members of the staff are employed by the firm and others by the Education Authority, and there are even instances in which the grant received by the Education Authority is partly or entirely handed over to the firm. It thus becomes a little difficult to define exactly the term 'Works Day Continuation School'.

If space permitted it could be shown that even when the general education of those under eighteen has been provided for—by the Local Education Authority, if you will—there is still plenty of other educational activity open to the enterprising employer who is prepared to carry on a Works School. The training of apprentices, trade and office classes, semi-recreative classes of all kinds—anything, in fact, which the employees of the firm sufficiently desire—can well be included in the programme of the Works School. Added to these is the whole question of the selection of employees by educational tests or on educational grounds, a matter which in most factories and business houses has hardly yet begun to be thought of.

Apropos of selection by tests may be mentioned the simple examination set by the Works Education Department to the boys applying for employment, some of whom afterwards make their appearance in the classes described in Chapter IV to VII. This examination serves various purpose. It shows, of course, which boys should not be taken on at all, but it is also a valuable factor in the classification of those employed when they are drafted into the Day Continuation School, and into various parts of the factory.

There is no room in this volume for even a selection of the quaint things sent in on these occasions, but one must express some curiosity as to the subsequent historical studies of the youth who assured the writer that 'Lord Kitchener was a famous Admiral, who won the battle of Waterloo.'

Undoubtedly the entrance examination for new employees is quite a useful institution, but something of much greater importance and value than an examination can be devised to form a connecting link between the school and the factory. The experiment of a Preparatory or Initiation School has been tried, having been brought within the limits of practicability by the new arrangement under which boys and girls leave the Day School at the end of the term only. A group of boys or girls, newly taken on, constitutes for—say—a week this Preparatory School. The pupils receive guidance on many matters referring to their future work, on health, cleanliness, use of leisure, works institutions, what to do and what to avoid—the instruction being as practical and realistic as possible. The lantern and the kinematograph may be brought into use, together with illustrative visits to show the chief processes carried on in the factory, the nature and sources of the raw materials, the properties and ultimate destinations of the finished products. While the girls learn to cut out their working overalls, the boys can be making plans of some simple parts of the building (from measurements taken by themselves). The time-table is varied by organised games, and observations which will bring out some of the main characteristics of the boy or girl. Should there be a superfluity of labour at the beginning of the new school term, this Preparatory School may with advantage be continued, on a diminishing scale, and on a part-time basis, for several weeks, thus forming a reserve to be drawn upon as required. Experience already gained seems to indicate that boys and girls enjoy this school. The premises of the Youths' Club and the Girls' Club can be readily adapted for the purpose, while a generously staffed factory has no difficulty in providing the necessary teachers. Of course, the pupils are paid for the time spent in this way, and the Preparatory School is distinct in every way from the Continuation School.

E. SOME PRACTICAL POINTS IN WHICH THE WORKS EDUCATION DEPARTMENT HELPS THE CONTINUATION SCHOOL

Speaking generally of the relation between the Day Continuation School and the employer it may be stated emphatically that time and trouble are well spent on friendly co-operation and the adjustment of difficulties and grievances on both sides, especially at the beginning of each school term. Any reasonable employer or foreman wishes the boys or girls to benefit as much as possible from attendance at school, as an indirect compensation for the encroachments made on the working week. The classification of Day Continuation School students into groups or sections may easily become complicated. It should not be entirely on the basis of educational attainment: age and temperament come into it also. One Standard VII boy of fourteen may be a child when compared with another of similar standard and age, whose additional stock of worldly wisdom has not been acquired altogether at school. It follows that, for a variety of reasons, there should be numbers of classes, approximately parallel in attainment but differing somewhat in other respects and meeting at various parts of the school week. Incidentally this segregation into groups often allows the head master or head mistress to offer the employer alternative times for the attendance of a particular student—a point of the utmost value, but one which can only be fully developed if the school is of fair size, say 400 or 500 students. Most differences in the placing of a boy or girl can be readily adjusted by a little compromise on both sides, but there is always the danger that the student's prospect of successful study may be compromised as well.

Adolescent girls seem to be peculiarly susceptible to accelerating or retarding influences caused by class environment, and we must generally reckon with the girl who steadily refuses to do her best unless her particular friend—for the moment—is in the same class.

What is the best way of dividing up our eight hours per week? To this question there can be no general answer, because so much depends on the nature of the industry in which the students are engaged, and on the mode of organisation of the school. The three main suggestions are: *(a)* one full day per week of approximately eight hours' study; *(b)* two half-days per week; *(c)* several shorter periods. In a general manufacturing concern it is quite likely that arrangement *(a)* causes less dislocation than any other. It is, however, educationally bad and only under exceptional circumstances (for example, in the case of students who work in a very dirty industry) should it be permitted. On the other hand, arrangement *(c)* causes unnecessary interruption to work in most factories, but in a distributing business such as a large retail warehouse—probably also in a small shop—where there are slack times on most days of the week, it is quite a convenient arrangement. This is true, particularly, if the school is on the same premises as the business, so that walking time and changing time are minimised. For the *average* student and *average* employer there seems no doubt that arrangement *(b)*—two distinct half-days per week—is more advantageous than any other. (Rural schools are not considered here.)

Should the Local Authority of the district decide to arrange its schools on a residential rather than an industrial basis, the position is somewhat different and then arrangement *(a)* has more to recommend it; but in most towns it will be found better to distribute the Day Continuation School students geographically according to their places of employment rather than according to their places of residence.

A simple mode of procedure which has been found helpful may be mentioned here.

At the beginning of each session, in a school already established, it is well for the head master or head mistress to be furnished by the employer with a complete list of juniors who will attend school, the list to be arranged departmentally and freely annotated. The notes will cover as many as possible of the special departmental and personal difficulties, even apparently trivial points being worth mentioning. To take actual examples, we find such remarks as 'Jane Smith and Susan Jones should attend on different days, if at all possible'; 'It upsets the work of this department if boys go to school on Friday morning'; 'Morning school preferred in this room'; and so on. Some three weeks before the commencement of the Autumn term this list goes to the head master or head mistress, then in the throes of planning time-tables. In, say, a week the list of classes or sections for each half-day comes to the Works Education Office, where it is analysed departmentally and tabulated. A sectional list in ten columns to correspond with the ten half-days is issued to each foreman or forewoman. The following is extracted from the covering letter sent with this table, as it reflects the spirit in which the arrangements are made between the school and the heads of departments, with the Works Education Office as a sort of clearing house.

> 'We have recently applied to the Day Continuation School a list of juniors in your Department, together with notes on how the girls could best be spared and on cases where it was difficult for two or more individual girls to attend together. While the classification has to be mainly on educational grounds an effort has been made to meet departmental difficulties. The lists of classes have now been received and the proposed time-table for your Department is sent herewith. If it is very inconvenient to spare any of the girl, at the times stated, please communicate at once with the Works Education Department. Any alteration generally means placing a girl in

a section which is less suitable for her than the one stated on the enclosed list.'

To minimise the inconvenience caused by all juniors in factory, or in a certain department of a factory, leaving work to attend school, there is no single universal remedy. Each factory, and even each department, has its own peculiar difficulties in this matter, which may be more or less removed by methods applicable to particular cases. A few illustrative cases may be taken. Department 'A' has eleven girls of day school age, but three are described as 'Head girls on machines' and no two of these can be spared out of the department at the same time: the other eight may, within reasonable limits, attend at any time. Department 'B' has forty-four girls in nineteen groups and no two from any one group may attend at the same time; there are also twenty-three other girls who can themselves be spared for school at almost any part of the week and whose duty it is to understudy girls in these nineteen groups and fill the vacancies caused by absence from the department. Another department, again, has ninety-six juniors, but it makes little difference to their work when they go to school, so long as the distribution throughout the week is fairly uniform. Special features are shown in departments where boys as well as girls are of school age; where work must be entirely cleared up by the week-end to avoid deterioration of unfinished goods during Saturday afternoon and Sunday; where a fall in output keeps another department waiting; where a junior habitually assists a senior; or where boys and men work together in groups or gangs and the work of the latter is held up by the absence of the former.

A system of relief boys or relief girls may have to be established and, if the factory is a large one, a possible method is to staff one department mainly with young boys or girls who can spend part of their week in other departments, taking the place of those who have gone to school. Of course the work of the relief room itself must be such that no serious loss is caused by a daily fluctuation in the staff. For instance, it had better be a department where the juniors work individually and not in groups. Some firms, having tried this plan, declare that it is not at all a desirable arrangement.

It has frequently happened—especially during the War—that in a room a particular operation can only be carried out by boys who have reached a certain height or a certain standard of physical development or intelligence. This is of common occurrence among boys in their last year of attendance at school, i.e., between seventeen and eighteen. (In the experiment here described each student who has not become eighteen before January 1 of a given year continues to attend school until July of that year, though in the case of boys this rule was temporarily modified by the operations of the Military Service Acts: Clause 10 of the Education Act provides differently and assumes that the fourth year of attendance at the Day Continuation School may be an incomplete school year.) If there are, say, three such youths in a room it is probably too much to expect the foreman to release all three, or even two of them, for school at once, but he can probably manage with two working while one area time goes to school.

In this connection it would be very interesting to follow out the case of the small employer, particularly in the case of the shopkeeper with only one or two juniors in his employment, or the mistress of a house with only one young domestic servant. In the Education Act, apparently power is given to the Local Authority not merely to specify the school which the student shall attend, but also to state definitely the particular hours or half-days of attendance. In many instances this will cause extreme inconvenience if the Local Education Committee takes full advantage of its powers without in any way consulting the employer. In very many cases there will be certain half-days much mere suitable than others from the employer's point of view, and a little toleration on both sides will do much to ensure that the employer is a sympathetic co-operator in the working of the Act and not a passive resister. At the same time it should be expressly stipulated that one of the two half-days should in all cases be a morning. Anyone who has had experience of teaching in a Day Continuation School knows how much better the work is done during a morning than during an afternoon, when the boy or girl has already put in four or five hours in the shop or factory—possibly with a special stimulus to activity on that half-day, 'because you go to school this afternoon'.

As the general movement towards a shorter working week proceeds, it will be found more and more that the afternoon half-day at school finishes at an hour later than that at which many places of employment have closed for the day. For example, in a factory with a 44-hour week junior employees may in the ordinary course go home at 5 o'clock. If an adequate mid-day interval is allowed and the afternoon classes commence at—say—1.45, they will naturally terminate at 5.45. Should the students be paid for the additional three-quarters of an hour or should they have time off at some other part of the day to compensate, or should they themselves make this comparatively small contribution towards the time given for study?

It is of the utmost importance that an employers should receive daily returns of absence and lateness, and on the form used for this purpose space should be left for special comments or suggestions. It is the duty of the Works Education Department to deal with these returns immediately they are received, to investigate the reasons for absence or unpunctuality, and report within a day or two to the head master or head mistress of the school.

Terminal or yearly reports are also essential if intimate co-operation is to be maintained between the firm and the school. These may be expressed partly in numerical form, giving the details of marks gained for term work, home work and examinations (examination marks should not appear too largely in the total, and should not exceed twenty-five per cent of the whole), and partly in verbal criticisms which represent the collective opinion of the members of the school staff.

If the school report is to be of any value it must be fully made use of by the employer, and this can be done in several ways. First: if there should be any system of rewards or prises given by the firm, this should be in a great measure based on the school reports, combined, if thought fit, with departmental reports. The latter, however, are apt to be fallacious, because the foreman or forewoman, although probably quite a competent head of his or her department, is not usually skilled in assessing merit on a numerical basis, and furthermore, the standard is apt to vary enormously between one department and another. A very kind-hearted foreman has been known to give everyone in his shop full marks, which is clearly unfair to the juniors who work for more discriminating heads. A perfectly fair and equitable basis for a general reward scheme is difficult to discover, because all sorts of allowances have to be made for age, occupation, temperament, environment, and the personal equation of the head of the department.

Of course, many educationists entirely condemn rewards of this kind, but if the reward takes the form of time and opportunity for more extended study surely most critics will be disarmed.

A second method of utilising school reports is to have them produced wherever wages are revised or selections made for more desirable posts. This method operates more through the association of ideas than in any direct way. It is well for progress at school and advancement at work to be linked up in the minds of the students. A third method, applicable to small groups of employees, and particularly to those who have received bad reports, is for the works educational official and the head of the student's department to talk over with the student the special points in his report and indicate possible improvement.

Conduct, as well as progress, may very well come under review on these occasions; in fact this is one of the most efficient methods by which the employer can help the head of the school in maintaining a satisfactory standard of discipline and behaviour.

The staff of the school and also the firm's representatives should be in frequent communication regarding boys or girls who do not seem to be happily placed as regards their work, or who show exceptional ability in some particular direction, or who seem worthy of appointment to some more desirable position, such as apprenticeship to a skilled trade. The Works Doctor can often be called into consultation with great advantage, especially at the present time when medical inspection of schools is not extended to Day Continuation Schools. Exemptions from home work, or from physical training, or even in rare cases from attending school altogether, may be granted on the doctor's recommendation.

If a promising student has been discovered, either by the school staff or by the Works Education Department, he or she should receive every encouragement. This may sometimes take the form of additional time at school, to enable the student to do more advanced work. In two actual cases, youths of about seventeen years of age were granted permission to attend (without loss of wages) continuation school on five half-days per week, instead of two, from January to Mid-summer. As a direct result of this special arrangement both students were successful in passing the intermediate examination for the B.Sc. degree of Birmingham University. Probably few persons realise the standard to which it is possible to raise the work of Day Continuation Schools, granted sufficient, time and a well-qualified and enthusiastic staff. Closely connected with arrangements such as this, there is the offer of scholarships to places of higher education, and these places are not necessarily technical schools. On the contrary, they may be colleges or settlements for higher study of quite non-vocational character, and even colleges of university rank. Co-operation with the Workers' Educational Association may well be undertaken at this stage.

In many matters affecting the *management* of the Day Continuation School it is reasonable to expect that firms keenly interested in eduction—and there are plenty of such firms—will wish to have some voice. To give effect to this, the Local Authority can readily co-opt representatives of these firms on the Bodies of Managers or Visitors, or on some Advisory Committee or Continuation School Sub-Committee.

On details of curriculum the teachers may with advantage consult the firms contributing large numbers of students, more especially as many industrial concerns have now at their disposal the services of experienced educational officials. There is no reason to fear that the advice of the employer will, in the vast majority of cases, be other than helpful. The more thoroughly the school and the employer appreciate one another's points of view, the better for all parties concerned, students included.

The critical reader of this chapter will doubtless say that all these arrangements demand from the employer much expenditure of time and money; this is quite true. In the scheme described in this volume the employers' part occupies the services of a full-time education official)(acting in conjunction with a Works Education Committee) and an education office staff, comparable with that required for the higher education of a moderate-sized town. But if the thing is worth doing at all it is worth doing well, and the opinion is steadily taking form among progressive employers that a highly organised educational scheme is an important and even essential adjunct to a large modern business. It would be interesting to follow the question up in two directions: first, to see how the work of the Day Continuation School can be supplemented by vocational and other specialised classes in the Works School; second, to discuss provision made for further educating employees of all ages, but these two subjects are probably outside the scope of this book.

10

Social Education

The focus of this chapter is the 'how' of Social Education Literature. As a first step towards it, we should examine the 'what' and the 'how' of Social Education itself. The same process of analysis suggests or first examining "Education" and "Social", each by itself. We may then find out the content of the compound "Social Education". This will give the answer to the 'what'. We may thereafter pursue the 'how'.

EDUCATION

"Education" is often taken to be an assumed term. This leads to difficulties. Education is not a sensory experience. It is not a concrete entity. It is an intellectual experience. It is essentially conceptual. It is the result of a certain amount of abstraction from diverse concrete experiences. Moreover, education has many facets. It can be viewed from diverse angles. Of these we have to choose a helpful facet and angle of approach. A helpful angle of approach presents education as a process. It is the process of development of personality. The personality of an individual is a holistic concept. It is not a mere assemblage of several elements. And yet, without forgetting this essential fact, we have as a preliminary step, to examine each of its constituents severally. For our purpose, we may recognise five sheaths in personality—vital, emotional, conational, intellectual and spiritual. We shall first examine each of these in turn.

Vital Sheath

The vital sheath (=living body) originates under the force of heredity. It is then subjected to the force of environment. The most influential part of the environment is nourishment. Shelter and clothing come next in order. But the supply of nourishment, shelter and clothing, is not by itself sufficient to help the development of body. Physical exercise is a necessary supplement. It is not usual to include the supply of food, shelter and clothing among the obligations of the agencies of education. These are taken to fall in the sphere of agencies in charge of public health and economics.

Physical Exercise

However, physical exercise has always been regarded as falling within the purview of education. It is true that adequate attention was not paid to it till very recently. This was due largely to the social and physical environment prevailing in those ties. Till a century or two ago, most of the countries had a rural set-up. In a rural set-up the density of population is low. Fresh air, freedom of movement, allurement by free space, plants and animals provided adequate opportunity for active physical life. Further, practically everybody had to take part in extracting the materials for food, shelter and clothing from nature. This also implied adequate physical movement. Physical exercise was thus a concomitant to the very process of living in rural setting except when within the grip of a disease. These simple conditions, with automatic provision for physical exercise, no doubt began to melt away after the setting in of industrialisation and the consequent drift towards cities. But the inertia of habit has delayed the recognition of the need for bringing physical exercise within the purview of education, after the emergence of urbanisation. However, nobody now denies the obligation of the agency of education to care for physical exercise.

Nutrition

Till the advent of compulsory education, nutrition was not taken to be within the purview of schools. The reason for this is obvious. The pupils were largely drawn from families in economic strata providing adequately for the nutrition of their members. Compulsory education changed this factor. At first failure of some children in absorbing school instruction was traced solely to their mental backwardness—so-called ineducability. In due course, under-nourishment came to be recognised as a possible cause. This led to the movement for the free supply of mid-day meal, milk and other forms of nourishment by the agencies of education.

The Butler Education Act, enacted in Great Britain during the years of the Second World War, gave legislative approval and sanction for this practice. But even here the responsibility is shared by the agencies for education as well as for health. The interest of the educational agency in the matter is only indirect. It is only to secure basic bodily fitness to accept teaching.

Force of Heredity

We have so far examined the jurisdiction of educational agencies in manipulating the force of environment in a way favourable to the development of the vital sheath. We should next examine the manipulation of the force of heredity. The force of heredity acts prior to the exit of the body from the mother's womb. It is obvious that no traditional agency of education can manipulate it. Indeed its manipulation lies, if at all, within the sphere of eugenics. Eugenics manipulates the individual not so much in the interest of his own development as in the interests of the individuals of the future generation. There are great difficulties in the free application of eugenical method. Modern development in X-rays and other rays at the left end of the spectrum of radiation, and the modern discovery of chemicals—all capable of hitting the gene and transforming it—are providing the means for manipulating the hereditary force. But there is still scepticism in the ultimate benefit of such a manipulation of the hereditary force. Nor are the scientific methods sufficiently advanced to overcome such a scepticism leading to abundant caution. Some success in changing a group within a few generations, by such methods, has been achieved in regard to laboratory organisms like banana fly. But we do not appear to have yet found methods guaranteeing such changes to be ultimately beneficial. Thus even eugenics is not able to achieve much in helping the development of the vital sheath of an individual. Therefore no case has been made as yet for education allying with eugenics, to bring the manipulation of the hereditary force within the jurisdiction of education.

The Other Sheaths

Emotion, conation and intellect are psychological entities. Each of them has a correlate in the physical body—glandular system and hormones; muscular system, afferent nervous system and roots of it in the brain chamber; the brain chamber including the roots of the efferent nervous system, the memory storing experiences, and the intellect building new experiences with the aid of those already stored in memory; respectively. Hardly anything is known about the physiological correlate of intuition (=the process of direct experience unmediated by sensory organs and intellect—mystical experience–spiritual experience). Educational agencies can do much to help the development of the emotional, conational and intellectual sheaths. The help often takes the form of providing models for imitation, and a carefully graded system of exercises. This amounts to manipulating the environment. Indeed the development of these sheaths is mostly a matter of reaction to environment. The essential element of the environment in this matter is the social one.

Emotional Sheath

It is usual to recognise two groups of emotions—lower and higher. An objective in education is the sublimation of lower emotion into its higher correlate—for example, love of oneself or selfishness into universal love; anger against trivial personal occurrences against oneself into indignation against serious social occurrences; and happiness derived from physical comfort into joy derived from creative work and into delight derived from spiritual realisation. Such a sublimation amounts to the development of the emotional sheath.

Educational Methods

Diverse methods are employed to help this development. The most effective method is that of providing examples for imitation. At any rate one has always to begin with this method. It is helpful also to end with it. A second method is that of precepts. Precepts can be made acceptable in diverse ways—by exercise of authority; by enforcing sanctions; and by reasoning. Social pressure often acts as an unperceived, inexorable authority. There is a danger here due to social pressure being the mere average of social practice. It cannot therefore produce the best of results. Sanction in the form of punishment had been long in vogue. Punishment used to take the form of corporal punishment and/or social ostracism. This method is now recognised to be undesirable. Such a cure often proves worse than the disease. Already the State has begun to prohibit sanctions of these sorts in the sublimation of emotions. The method of reasoning may not be effective in the case of all. Very involved reasoning may be necessary, in some cases, to carry conviction. In extreme cases this will work only with intellectuals. This remark about the method of precepts does not amount to a denial of the efficacy of the method. On the other hand, it merely emphasises the insufficiency of the method of precepts by itself. In other words, it is necessary but not sufficient. A judicious coupling of the method of example and the method of precepts is the most effective educational method in helping the development of the emotional sheath.

Chemical Methods

The sublimation of emotion has also been attempted in the past by chemical methods. This method is based on the close correlation of emotions and hormones. This correlation is now being studied intensively. It is now granted that there is a specificity in the emotion-harmone relation. Every emotion stimulates the discharge of its harmone-correlate. The chemical method is based upon the converse process. It is believed that the stimulation of the discharge of a hormone can produce its emotion-correlate. The whole process of addiction is now being sought to be explained along these lines. One school of practitioners of depth-psychology resorts to the application of chemical methods. But kick-back residual reactions are believed to be injurious. Repetition is believed to lead even to permanent injury. Opium-eaters and chain-smokers are examples. On the contrary I have heard reports from reliable friends of mine—high in the scale of spiritual experience—about the efficacy of chemical methods as starter, so to speak. The *Ramayana* and the *Mahabharata* describe its efficiency. According to tradition, the "Siddhas" of India were adepts in the use of this method. According to them an adept is required to apply this method in safe doses and frequencies. But adepts are so few in number. Moreover they are very strict in administering their methods. They are prepared to administer them only in very few cases. They regard all other cases to be unfit for the administration of this method. The chemical method cannot therefore come into wide practice. The development of the emotional sheath has therefore to depend largely on educational methods.

Inertial Emotion

In addition to lower and higher emotions, we have also to recognise a third group. I call this group one of inertial emotions.

It is made of the lowest form of pleasure derived from inertia, inaction, indolence, passive listening to gossip, or at best from active participation in gossiping. This lowest form of emotion is often widely prevalent among degenerate vanishing tribes. It is also generally prevalent in a community passing through the phase of cultural exhaustion. It has been so in the Indian community during the last few centuries. Even in a community in the active phase of its cultural cycle, intertial emotion may possess some individuals. Physical disorder—dull lever, for example—may be the cause for indulgence in inertial emotion. Then, a physical cure is necessary. But intertial emotion may persist even without any physiological correlate. In that case emotional development is inhibited or obstructed. It is the duty of educational agency to remove the obstruction. The methods available for it are similar to those available for the sublimation of lower emotions to higher ones.

Conational Sheath

Conation or will is a potent mental factor. The development of will is one of the most neglected fields in education. Will may receive its drive from any of the other sheaths. Without its development every other sheath may wither away.

Relation to Vital Sheath

The urge for food, clothing or shelter often stimulates will. This stimulus to will is believed to be compelling and universal. There are, however, cases when even hunger had failed to set up sufficient will-power. Sometimes will is exercised to bear with hunger.

Relation to Emotional Sheath

The reciprocity of relation is more balanced between the emotional sheath and the conational sheath. A non-inertial lower emotion—like anger, hatred and passion of every other sort—is impulsive in its nature. It exercises great pressure over a short duration. Its impulsive pressure often turns the trigger. It stimulates will. Action follows. But the action also is impulsive. It is of great intensity. It is finished in a moment. It is not sustained. Action due to will stimulated by a lower emotion is seldom lasting. Will depending on a lower emotion is discontinuous. It is perhaps even involuntary. It cannot be controlled. It cannot be regulated. It cannot be invoked at pleasure, so to speak. On the other hand, will can be so developed as to control lower emotions. In fact sublimation of a lower emotion to its higher correlate has to depend on the exercise of will. Development of the conational sheath is therefore necessary for the development of the emotional sheath. A higher emotion always ensures developed will. In fact, after a certain stage of development, development of the emotional sheath keeps step with that of the conational sheath. This stage is a critical point in the development of personality—in education. After crossing this critical point, it is usually smooth sailing. Formal educational agencies usually neglect the development of will as well as emotion even upto this critical point.

Relation to Intellectual Sheath

The reciprocity between the conational and the intellectual sheaths is of a poor sort. The development of will is necessary for the development of intellect. But it is not sufficient. On the other hand, the development of intellect is neither necessary nor sufficient for the development of will. Most of the tragedy of the university-educated men in India today is the tragedy of under-developed will to execute the findings of developed intellect. The most virulent element in the social pathology of India's intellectual class today is weak will. The irony is the exercise of the very intellectual power to explain away the results of weak will. I have known much respected highly evolved intellectuals honestly justifying their inertia by extremely clever arguments. When faced with such arguments, I have often found myself out of wits to controvert them All the same the mockery—may the tragedy—of the situation has always been unmistakable. Such situations induce a deep sense of sorrow in me.

A Devastating Happening

The conscious development of intellect and the total neglect of the development of will by our educational agencies lead to devastating results of a far reaching kind. The intellectuals, the educated folk, and the university-turned individuals possess a powerful tool in their hands to make plans of all kinds, to speak to the masses in all sorts of appealing styles, and to entrench themselves in advantageous positions. They do not have the will to carry out the plans conjured by their intellect, or to carry out the promises glibly made by them or to pay back to the community in a worthy form the advantages derived by them in their entrenched positions. In fact it makes many of the intellectual folks fail to satisfy the Shavian definition of a gentleman—one who never takes more from society than what he is able to give back. It requires great will to be a gentleman. But alas! our educational agencies do precious little to develop will.

Educational Method

Unlike in the case of the development of the vital or emotional sheath, there appears to be hardly any method other than educational method to develop will. There is no nutritional method, for example, nor is there a chemical method. The responsibility of educational agencies in the development of will is all the greater.

Very little is now known of the technique of developing will. This is due to the long neglect of this function by educational agencies. The ancient Tamil classics give pictures of the methods used to develop will. The Spartans have the reputation of having devoted much thought to the technique of developing will. People in the grip of lower emotions develop great will for the moment. War-hysteria develops enormous will in a whole nation. Recent study of hysteria has shown the possibility of the increase of muscular strength to nearly a hundred times the normal one. Muscular strength is one of the psychological correlates of conational strength. The above-mentioned result about hysteria proves the potential capacity of the body to stand the strain of highly developed will. Apart from that, the wisdom of inducing hysteria—by fear, avarice, hatred or passion of any kind—is doubtful. Research on the correct technique of developing the conational sheath in a steady beneficient way, without any damaging after-effect, is yet to be done. It is high time that it is done. For it looks as if the great opportunity for self-development provided for us by Mahatma Gandhi will slip away for want of developed will in most of us.

Intellectual Sheath

All along, formal and conscious education had been concentrated on the development of the intellectual sheath of personality. Physical development was largely left to the casual care of the family. Emotional development was similarly left to the casual influence of the family and the community.

Development of the will was never consciously attempted. But development of the intellect has always been the centre of attention in educational process. Several techniques have been developed for this work. Before enumerating them it may be a convenience to examine the process of intellectual development—the sharpening of intellect and the enrichment of intellectual experience. It is generally believed that thinking, memory and sensory experience are inseparably connected with language. Language is of course necessary for the communication of experience between members of a community. Its being necessary for communion with oneself appears to compel equal acceptance. Indeed, in a sense, the process of intellectual development is a correlate of the development of Thought-Term Relation in one's mind. The ineffectiveness of teaching is often traceable to neglect of the difference in Thought-Term Relation between the teacher and the taught. This ineffectiveness, I have often noted even in a small homogeneous class pursuing a narrow subject. I used to check it up now and again. The ineffectiveness will be even more pronounced in a bigger and less homogeneous class. Thus making Thought-Term Relation precise is essential in the process of teaching. Further, intellectual development and formation of Thought-Term Relation are inseparable. It is therefore worthwhile to examine this question in greater detail, as a preliminary measure. Experience can be one of three categories. The same is true of term also. Here are the three categories:

(1) Sensory experience dominantly of a vital on sensory origin;

(2) Intellectual experience dominantly of an intellectual or logical origin, without the intervention of sensory experiences in the process of thinking except before beginning the inference stage; and

(3) Mystic or intuitive experience unmediated by sensory or intellectual experiences in the process of intuiting.

Brain-Chamber

The accompanying schematic diagram will be an aid in the further discussion of this matter. Brain is the chamber. The primary senses are the windows in its walls. Memory is the reservoir in it. Intellect is the vessel for cooking thought. Logic is the fire used in cooking. The sensory nerves are the inlet pipes leading from the windows into the reservoir and pouring pure sensory experience into memory. There is a pipe for flow from the reservoir into the vessel. There is another pipe for flow from the vessel into the reservoir.

BRAIN (CHAMBER)

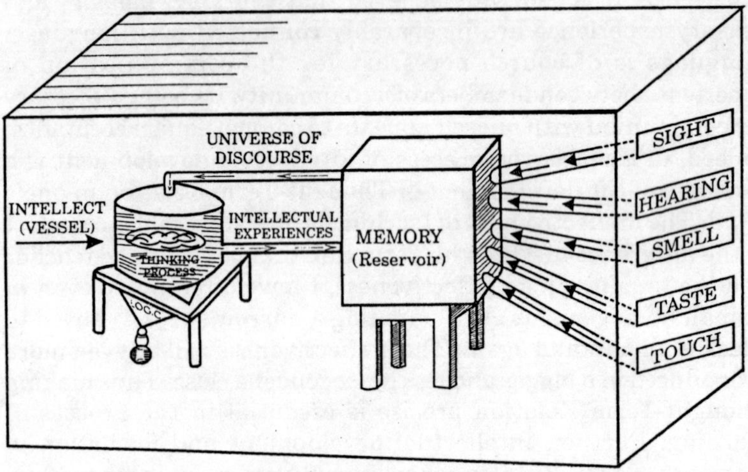

Sensory Experience and Term

Pure sensory experience is unspeakable. In other words, there can be no pure sensory term. This is the same as saving that a sensation stimulated by an entity outside the skin through the medium of the primary senses—*e.g.*, sight, hearing, smell, touch, taste—is unspeakable. It has first to be repeated, stored in memory, recalled from it, tallied with a fresh pure sensory experience, and the latter declared to be like or unlike it. It is only after the completion of this process within the brain, that a pure sensory experience becomes speakable. In other words, it is only then that it gets represented by a term in the verbal plane. The above-mentioned process within the brain is intellectual and not sensory. Therefore, strictly speaking, there can be no pure sensory term. In what follows the term 'Sensory Term' is used only to denote a term which gets coined with the aid of a minimum of intellectual process.

Educational Method

The educational method for developing sensory efficiency has been considerably improved during the last 50 years. Hand and eye training, manual training and laboratory methods are the result. In the first place, the capacity of the primary senses is itself improved. Competence is also secured in the use of tools, instruments and other aids to intensify the capacity of the senses. Practice rather than precept is the chief feature of this technique.

Intellectual Experience

Intellect is the vessel within the brain. Some of the contents of the memory are passed into it. These are picked up in various combinations. The entities in these combinations are permuted, alloyed, fused, integrated and so on—cooked, so to speak—within the intellect. This is thinking. The result is an intellectual experience as distinct from sensory experience. Three stages can be recognised in thinking:

(1) Assumption;

(2) Inference; and

(3) Verification.

Assumption—The assumption-stage of thinking consists of picking out from memory an assortment of sensory experiences—ancient, recent or nascent. The respective sensory terms come up as correlates. Rigorous thinking should pick up all the necessary sensory experiences and terms at the very outset. Even if it is obliged to admit new-comers while in the second stage, they should be recognised as new-comers and admitted with full awareness. If their admission needs any re-examination of the second stage of thinking already done, it should be forthwith done. The first stage of thinking is 'empirical'. The combination of experiences collected together before the second stage begins finally, is denoted by the term "Universe of Discourse". The term denoting any of these experiences is called "Assumed Term" if it denotes an individual experience and "Defined Term" if it denotes a combination of experienced.

Inference—The inference-stage of thinking consists of the rest of thinking—permutation and so on. This stage of thinking is "deductive". The whole of thinking—*i.e.,* assumption, plus interence—results in intellectual experience. An intellectual experience of a person is, in a sense, self-created *i.e.,* created within the intellect without interference, at the second stage of thinking, by entities outside it, be they from memory or from outside the skin. It is "valid" if it conforms to the rules of logic. Otherwise it is "invalid."

Verification—A valid intellectual experience is taken into memory for tallying. If the tallying succeeds in finding predecessor, it is "associated" within the memory. If no predecessor is found, it is tested and tallied with the happenings outside the skin. This is empirical. If the tallying is successful, the intellectual experience is accepted as "true", associated and named. Otherwise it is rejected as "false".

Expression, Sentence, Term—In the verbal plane an intellectual experience may, in some cases, require only a term to name it. It may, in other cases, require a sentence.

A sentence is a sequence of terms. Some of the terms are "substantives". Some are "connectives". Some substantives denote "things or objects". Some of them denote "attributes of things, or action". The sequence of terms is intelligible if it conforms to the rules of grammar. Otherwise it is "unintelligible".

If the sentence is intelligible and the intellectual experience expressed by it is true, it is "meaningful". Otherwise, it is "meaningless".

The different stages of thinking leading to an intellectual experience may require a series of sentences to be denoted. The term "expression" may be used to denote a term, a sentence or a series of sentences.

Abstract Term—Intellectual experience and term are said to be more abstract than sensory experience and term respectively. The experiences brought up at the assumption-stage of thinking may themselves be intellectual. The intellectual experience and term, got by ploughing back into the thinking process the intellectual experiences already stored in memory, are said to be more abstract than the intellectual experience and term used at the assumption stage of thinking. Thus every round of thinking may create a greater degree of abstraction. In any round of thinking, any experience and its term, brought up at the assumption stage is "assumed experience and term", relative to that round of thinking irrespective of its being sensory or intellectual.

Assumed Term—A term bringing an experience—sensory or intellectual—within apprehension, spontaneously and instantaneously with a minimum of associative effort among the members of a group of people, is an "Assumed Term" for that group.

Educational Method—A proper technique was evolved, earliest in the history of education, for the imparting of the methods of correct thinking. These methods were developed as an adjunct to the study of philosophy. The study of philosophy is as old as man. Therefore the method of teaching thinking may also be taken to be as old as man. The method consisted both of example and precept. As usual one has to begin with example. One has to involve the innate tendency of imitation to as full an extent as possible. The process of imitation begins early in life—even in pre-school days. It goes on continuously. Precepts are taught only at a later stage. Some maturity born out of practice is necessary for the method of precepts to become effective.

Memory

Memory is thus a reservoir of sensory and intellectual experiences and terms. In respect of memory, man differs essentially from animals. An animal can have its memory enriched only by its own experience. In other words it is time-bound. It cannot enrich its memory with the experiences stored in the memory of its ancestors or fully even of its contemporaries. On the contrary, man can do so. In other words, his memory is not time-bound. One consequence of this is that the experiences to be carried in memory go on increasing from generation to generation. Here is a rough list of the major inventions of a single generation:

1892	Automatic telephone patented.
1892	Internal combustion engine invented.
1894	Typhoid anti-toxin and diphtheria anti-toxin introduced
1895	X-rays discovered.
	Principles of the motor car patented.
1896	Steam turbine patented.
	First cinema show.
1897	Electrons identified.

1898 Radium discovered.
1899 Long distance telephone invented.
'Sugar' prune developed.
1900 Gasoline motor invented.
Submarine invented.
1901 Wireless signals flashed across the Atlantic. High speed steel invented.
1902 Active emanations of radium identified.
1903 Ford-car patented.
First flight of 120 feet in 12 seconds.
1904 Fessenden's plan of radio-wave production patented.
1905 Theory of relativity announced.
1906 Crystal detector patented.
1907 Vitamin hypothesis postulated.
1908 Two and a half miles of continuous flying.
1909 Installation of wireless in steamship.
1910 Ionic medication invented
1911 Hydro-air plane invented.
1912 Talking pictures invented.

All these inventions have already come to affect our daily life. Each connotes a large bunch of experiences to be stored in memory.

Externalised Memory—This staggering succession of inventions prove too many for memory. It can only take in and retain so much. It is impossible for the memory of any one to hold even a billionth part of what there is to be remembered. And yet any of us will have occasion to know and use any of the billion existing facts. To meet this dilemma humanity invented writing materials, printing and more recently a special class of books—reference books—to relieve memory of a considerable amount of its contents. Indeed a reference book is "externalised memory".

Verbal Testimony—The invention of articulate speech to express thought and the communication of expressed thought from man to man and from generation to generation, by word of mouth or by printed records have added a new source of experience—verbal testimony. This source is different from those of sensory and intellectual experiences. The experience emanating from this source may be called "Verbal Experience".

Education by Rote Memory—Rote-Memory is usually very efficient in the earlier years of life. It is not unusual to find children of nursery school stage repeating the whole of the *Gita*, the *Vishnu sahasranama* and *Krishna karnamrita*. These children obviously know the words. There is no Thought-Term Relation at all. It is possible that Thought-Term Relation may sprout years later. But often the contents of rote-memory evaporate before the development of Thought-Term Relation.

Memory without Education—Again a consequence of the absence of Thought-Term Relation in rote-memory, is the absence of no effect whatever of the memory on the conduct and life of the individual. In such a case development of memory does not amount to education. It is so even when thought-term relation is established without any effect on conduct and life. This has been repeatedly expressed all through the ages. One of the ancient records of this is in the *Chandogyopanishad*. A pathetic appeal of Narada in the words, "I have learnt the Vedas, the Itihasas, the Purans, the Arts, the Sciences and the Crafts. Still I do not feel educated. I am in grief. Pray, help me". Sanatkumara begins saying, "What you have learnt are only terms. You have merely stored them in your memory. They have not been integrated with your conduct and life."

Educational Method—For a long time, only rote memory was developed. The method used was repeating a passage several times. Marvels of memory had been developed in this way. All the Vedas, all the Itihasas, most of the Puranas, many Poems, Dramas, Dictionaries and other treatises had been stored in memory by many individuals. Even today there are persons with such a colossal memory to their credit. In recent years, the futility of rote memory has been realised. Attention is being paid to the development of associative and rational memory. Oft-required facts and pieces of knowledge are stored in memory. Education aims to enrich memory of oft-required facts and pieces of knowledge. These are so packed in memory to facilitate recall by association. This form of packing makes use of considerable reasoning. Recall by association also makes use of reasoning.

Use of Externalised Memory—Modern technique for the development of memory implies also development of the capacity to use externalised memory. Education for a changing world has now come to mean not merely imparting the pupils basic facts and pieces of knowledge but also teaching them the methods of finding out other facts and pieces of knowledge as and when needed. In other words the camel theory of education is no longer the dominant theory. The technique used in teaching methods of using externalised memory, consists of rousing curiosity in the pupil inducing an enquiring and exploring attitude, and providing him opportunities to make use of reference books, *i.e.*, externalised memory. This means creating situations in which the pupil has to find out many things by himself and not for the teacher to tell him everything; providing opportunities for finding them; throwing the pupil amidst books; guiding him to find his way about; training him in extracting the necessary elements from appropriate books; and teaching him to weave these elements into a whole so as to become the information required. Details of this technique are fully developed in Part 3 "How of School Libraries' of my *School and college libraries* (Madras Library Association, publication series, 11)1942.

Skills

Development of intellectual sheath implies development of diverse skills. These may be the so-called manual skills or mental skills. A skill is a holistic resultant of an assorted set of sensory, verbal and intellectual experiences. This resultant is dynamic. It can grow. It can pave the way for the development of associated skills. The technique for developing a skill is that of example and practice. It begins with imitating a model. The model may be a living one, or a mechanical one, or one expressed in words either as case-description or as rules of procedure. Thereafter, the skill has to be strengthened by continuous practice. This is true of all skills.

Spiritual Sheath

The development of the spiritual sheath is helped by the release of intuition (=building up experience unmediated by sensory organs or intellect). Intuition is known to be notoriously erratic. In Sambandar it got released at 3. In Appar it got released at 50. In Sankara it got released at 7. In Pattinattar it did not flair out till after middle age. The inner light blased forth in Christ and Buddha at the threshold of adolescence. It was delayed till about the fortieth year in Muhammad. In Ramanarishi intuition began to function when he was at school; in Sri Aurobindo it waited till he had been in service for some years. Therefore the furtherance of growth in the spiritual sheath is elusive. The soul eludes all. The technique for releasing intuition is not known. We can at best approach it by intensifying sensory and intellectual experiences. Intuitive experience may be regarded as a limiting point of a series of intellectual experiences. It does not, however, belong to this series. It is outside it. And yet it can be approximated to as closely as desired. One method of helping the release of intuition is to soke the mind with information about great souls—realised souls, saints, prophets, founders of religion, seers and rishis—all self-centres of light. One negative warning must be remembered. We should not mistake the teaching of creeds and rituals for soking the minds with information about great souls. Creeds and rituals are methods crystalised so as to suit certain cultural conditions. They often have a nucleus of essential and everlasting value. But this nuclear element is soon coated with an impenetrable incrustation. The more the creeds and rituals over-stay their time, the more opaque becomes the crust. Strictly speaking the development of the spiritual sheath is not amenable to ordinary educational method. For the effective force which acts on it is psycheo-genetic one. In Sanskrit tradition, it is called the force of *Vasana*. The soul carries the *Vasana* with it from embodiment to embodiment. It gets enriched and progressively sublimated in the onward march of the soul in its own evolution. The force of *Vasana* is too subtle for the so-called scientific measurement and manipulation, belonging to the intellectual sheath. Its very existence is questioned in orthodox educated cloisters. At best it is branded as something belonging to the occult. But the Indian tradition is alive to it. The *Adepts* recognise and isolate it. But even they often declare it to be beyond the reach of manipulation.

Whole Man

We have so far dwelt on the development of each of the sheaths in the personality of man. We must now recall to mind the remark about the holistic nature of education. The education of the whole man is not a mere arithmetical sum of the education of each of his sheaths. Nor is the education of the whole man achieved by educating each of his sheaths independently. Its achievement requires the simultaneous correlated education of each sheath. The correlation should be achieved in quantity, quality, and pace. In the past, there was little correlation. Most of the sheaths were neglected. The intellectual sheath alone occupied most of the attention. The result could have been truly disastrous. Disaster was averted by the attention of formal agencies of education being confined to men of intrinsically superior personality. The innate force of such a personality helped it to glide over the destructive shoals. It enabled it to emerge from the damage done by the grip of formal agencies giving faulty partial education. In a sense, then, such a superior personality educated himself in spite of his school and college rather than because of them. Such a righting of faults in education, by sheer life-force, cannot happen in the case of the less organised personalities now being brought into schools. Drifting in education must, therefore, be replaced by conscious and scientific work. John Dewey had emphasised this in his works on education. His *school and society* is a seminal book in regard to this matter. He demonstrated his ideas in his Experimental School. A swelling stream of new thought on education has been flowing since Dewey's initiation. For some time, the term "New Education" was used to emphasise the change. The change was towards education of the whole man.

Educational Method

Various educational methods are possible—Apprenticeship, Laboratory Workshop, Lecture, Seminar, Forum and Project. In the actual life-situation of the class room the method will be determined in an organic way by a triangle of forces—the personality, resourcefulness and ability of the teacher; the personality, capacity and mood of the pupils; the subject to be expounded or the skill to be developed, as the core, the extent of information to be imparted, the extent of sublimation of emotion to be attempted, and the extent of strengthening of will to be realised. The method will in this sense be unique. It can hardly be pre-determined. But for purposes of understanding it, we must analyse the synthetic whole into its elements. We should examine the value of each method severally and collectively. This preliminary analysis will help in improving the attitude and awareness to forge the right method on the spot by spontaneous synthesis and with magical effectiveness.

Apprenticeship

The term *Antevasi* (=one living in the immediate presence), used to denote a pupil in Indian tradition, emphasises the efficacy of the method of apprenticeship in learning any subject or skill whatever. In later cultural epochs apprenticeship was regularly used as a method to teach arts and crafts. This method presupposes the availability of a master to take the pupil under his care. In the Vedic tradition, the master was an adept. He had full insight into the peculiarities of all the sheaths in the personality of the pupil. His method was severely personal. It was also individualistic. The method used by sage Valmiki in educating the pupils Kusa, Lava and the others in his *ashram* (sylvan university centre), is depicted graphically in the drama *Uttara Rama carita.* It is a charming demonstration of the method of *antevasi.* In the application of apprenticeship method to arts and crafts, the master may not subordinate the economic interests of his business to the educational needs of his pupils.

Laboratory

The essential feature of the apprentice method is learning by doing. This element was in recent years separated from the concrete setting of apprenticeship. This separation reduced the rigour. It also provided greater opportunity for learning. This developed into the laboratory method. This method is applicable not only to arts and crafts but to all the sciences—using this term in a generalised sense.

Workshop

A recent variation of the laboratory method is the workshop method. Workshop is distinguished from the laboratory in its emphasis on the availability of the results of work for use. Consequently workshop method is more realistic. Mahatma Gandhi advocated it. He even went to the extreme of emphasising the possibility of solving the financial problem of the school by the adoption of workshop method, in the present conditions of India.

Lecture

Humanities lend themselves readily to the lecture method.

Its being independent of literacy extends its use widely. It still survives rightly in the education of illiterates. The non-English-educated scholars of South India have developed it as a fine art. It is called "Katha". They often know the basic books—the *Ramayana,* the *Bhagavata* and the other puranas—by heart. Some chapter is taken as the text for lecture. On that, is usually hung a good deal of matter of literary, religious, philosophical, historical, sociological and legal import. It is truly a criticism of life. The exposition is punctuated by wit and humour. Haranguing, singing and story-telling are alternated dexterously. But these charming features of effective lecture method have not been grafted to the modern mode of lecturing. With the result, the modern lecture soon becomes boring. The consequences of its inherent defect of keeping the audience passive get very pronounced.

Seminar

In the seminar method, pupils are formed into smaller groups. The groups are also made homogeneous in regard to interests, previous knowledge and capacity. A definite proposition is enunciated for each setting. The assumptions are explicitly started. A prior study of the problem is made by the members according to a prescribed bibliography. The pupils exchange their ideas under the guidance of the teacher. This develops team-spirit and self-reliance. Granted skill in the teacher in piloting the work, the seminar method is very effective. During the last two years, this is being experimented upon in the Department of Library Science of the University of Delhi. It brings out the innate capacity of the members. It develops awareness, alertness and participativeness. Above all it is entirely free from boredom.

Forum

The seminar method exploits the habit of discussion innate in man. Till the advent of the seminar method, this innate habit was not fully and properly utilised in education. It was running to waste by taking less profitable form like mere gossip. The seminar method harnesses the innate urge for discussion. It sublimates it into one of real value. The forum method is an improvement on the seminar method. A forum has been defined as an assembly of people gathered together for discussing specified subject by acknowledged leaders with full opportunity for participation by the audience. A forum consists of two stages—

address by one or more experts; and a question and discussion period. The audience take part in the second stage. The first stage of a forum may take various forms:—

Symposium—Three or more persons assumed to be authorities on different aspects of a subject deliver a brief address covering between themselves all the relevant aspects of the subject.

Panel—Three or more persons assumed to be able representatives of different views on a given subject engage in a discussion before the audience, in an attempt to clarify certain issues and points of difference.

Lecture-panel—A speaker presents an address following which a panel of three or more persons representing different points of view discuss the important points in the address among themselves and with the speaker.

Debate-panel—Same as the Lecture-panel in which two debaters take the place of a single lecturer.

Dialogue—Two persons, both experts, carry on a dialogue without set speech.

The forum method gives opportunity to the pupils to look before and around the subject of discourse. It encourages them to ask questions, to think out replies, and to venture into new ideas. There listening in the first stage is not merely passive. It is purposive and active.

Project Method

The project method synthesises all the other six methods. It impregnates education with a reality and an intimacy lacking in any other method taken severally. In this method, education goes very much on its own steam. It is carried forward in a natural way. Nothing is learnt in this method without the need for its immediate application. No lecture is attended, no work is done, and no book is read except under the urge to achieve something here and now. The motive force of interest is not hidden. Further it is nascent. The formative force of imitation finds full opportunity as in apprenticeship, laboratory work, workshop practice, lecture, seminar and discussion, forming part of it. The anticipatory pleasure of achieving something is a wholesome pull. The completion of a project by a group gives it an exhilarated and socialising experience.

This method is a recent invention. It has its roots in the movements started by John Dewey half a century ago. It develops team-spirit and self-reliance in abundance.

Library

The Library is auxiliary to each one of the seven methods discussed so far. A library is a social institution. In it properly organised books and other kindred materials and the readers are brought into purposeful, pleasureable and effective contract by a competent staff in a personal manner. Books being artificial entities, a special set of techniques is necessary—to get the books properly used; to find every reader his book; to find every books its reader; to save the time of the reader and for this purpose to save the time of the staff. These constitute library technique. Library service aims at helping readers to exploit the printed resources to the maximum extent possible. It seeks to train them to read books participatively and purposefully. It develops in them the art of taking notes, re-assembling them, and integrating them with their own thought-content. It trains pupils to work in the library for prior background study, parallel reading and follow-up work. The library helps pupils to come back to their difficulty again and again—as often as necessary—till it is removed. This opportunity given by the library respects the differences in the speed of learning of different pupils. Library work supplements apprenticeship, laboratory work and workshop practice. It enables pupils to follow lectures with interest. It feeds them to take part in the forum with confidence and enlightenment. It encourages self-dependence in projects, and widens the horizon of the pupils in every way. Indeed the library should be the hub of every educational institution. Every other work should be made to radiate from and be irradiated by the library. Of course the use of the library pre-supposes the existence of literature. As shown by its very title, the subject of this book is the production of literature needed for library work.

SOCIAL

We have so far considered education as a process pertaining to an individual. The epithet "social" applied to "education" would turn our attention either wholely or partly from the individual to his society, *i.e.*, community or group, and his relation to it.

"Social" is an over-worked term. As many-as 24 different shades of its meaning can be recognised. Here they are:

(1) *(Obs)*. Capable of being associated or united to others.

(2) (*Obs*). Associated

(3) (*Rate*) Occurring or taking place between allies.

(4) Marked or characterised by mutual intercourse, friendliness, or geniality.

(5) (*Obs*). Expressive of, proceeding from, sympathy.

(6) (*Obs*). United by common tie.

(7) Inclined to friendly intercourse; sociable.

(8) Consisting of persons associated together in friendly intercourse.

(9) Disposed to live in communities.

(10) Pertaining to society as an organism.

(11) Pertaining to institutions.

(12) Pertaining to rank.

(13) Pertaining to human beings in their physical contacts or to evils resulting from such contacts, as over-crowding, and especially venereal contagion.

(14) Pertaining to conditions in or the welfare of human society, especially in regard to a class or to classes below or likely to fall below the community standard of well-being, as the poor, the alien, the neglected, the mal-adjusted, the abnormal.

(15) Pertaining to social (sense 4) activities.

(16) Concerned with the constitution of society and the problems presented by this—of persons.

(17) Concerned with the constitution of society and the problems presented by this— of sciences.

(18) Socialistic or communistic: specifically pertaining to relations between capital and labour.

(19) Pertaining to corporation and partnership in law.

(20) Pertaining to primitive society.

(21) Reaching all members of society.

(22) Pertaining to the material welfre of society.

(23) Resulting from human activity.

(24) A combination of senses 14 and 18.

Inapplicable Meanings

Of the 24 meanings of "Social", five are obsolete or rare—meanings 1, 2, 3, 5 and 6. We may ignore them. Ten have no relevance to "education", actual or potential—meanings 4, 8, 11, 15, 16, 18, 19, 20, 23 and 24. We may ignore these also. For with any of these meanings, "social" cannot be meaningfully coupled with "education".

SOCIAL EDUCATION

The remaining nine meanings of "social" lend themselves to be coupled with "education" in a meaningful way. But usage has not yet so coupled them. We may, however, examine the possible meaning "social education" can have with each of these nine different meanings of "social". After examining each such combination, we shall also state whether this book uses "social education" in that sense or not.

Social Education—Sense 1

Six of the definitions refer to way of life, technique or science—meanings 7, 9, 12, 13, 16 and 17. If "social" in any of these senses is coupled with "education", the result will mean "Education in the particular way of life or technique or science". This combination does have a meaning. We have analogies for this. We use, for example, "Medical Education" to mean "Education in the medical fields of knowledge". On this analogy "Social Educaiton" can be taken to mean "Educaiton in the social fields of knowledge"—six fields implied in the six meanings corresponding to the six meanings of "social" referred to. In this connection we may say that according to current usage, "Social Sciences" includes subjects like Educaiton, History, Political Science, Economics, Sociology and Law. Therefore "Social Education" may mean training in any of these subjects. "Social Educaiton Literature", will then mean merely "Reading Materials in Social Sciences" or "Books on the Teaching of Social Sciences". In this book, we are not considering the production of either of these classes of reading materials. Therefore, we are not using "Social Educaiton" in sense 1.

Social Education—Sense 2

Giving "Social" the meaning 21, will make "Social Education" mean "Education Reaching All Members of Society". We have already a common term to denote it, *viz.* Universal Education. Since 1870 and till the Second World War, universal education was focussed on literacy—a mere means of self-educaiton through recorded thought. After the Second World War, emphasis was shifted from the means to the contents of universal education. To underline this change, the term "Fundamental Education" has been coined to denote the second possible sense of "Social Education". There can be literature fit to be used both by the educands and the educators of fundamental education—on its content as well as its methodology. And yet in this book we are not using either "Social Educaiton" in the sense of "Fundamental Education", or "Social Educaiton Literature" in the sense of "Fundamental Education Literature".

Social Education—Sense 3

Giving "Social" the meaning 10, will make "Social Education" mean "Education Pertaining to Society as Organism". In this meaning of "Social Education", "Social" may turn out to be tautological. For there is an accepted definition of "Education" itself, equivalent to this third sense of "Social Education". That accepted definition is a teleological one. Teleology, according to Bosanquet, is the operation of a conscious purpose entertained by human intelligence. What is the conscious purpose of education?

A minimum conscious purpose has been mentioned by John Dewey in his *Democracy and education* (Textbook series ed. by Paul Monroe) 1920. According to this purpose, "Education" signifies the sum total of processes by which a community or a social group, whether small or large, transmits its acquired powers with a view to securing its own continued existence. In the *Encyclopedia of social sciences* George S. Counts makes a similar enunciation. According to him, the main purpose of education is the induction of the maturing individual into the life of the group, the group being broadly conceived to include the dead as well as the living. This definition of "Education" itself is exactly sense 3 of Social Education. Therefore in this chapter "Social Education" is not used in the third sense.

Social Education—Sense 4

The purpose of education may be an ever widening one. Almost in every age, far-seeing men had criticised the narrowness of their contemporary view of the purpose of education. They had suggested their own alternative Utopian ideas. Later ages had actually realised many of the dreams of the earlier ages. Having done so, they have evolved a new Utopian idea in advance of their times for the still later ages to realise in their turn. Plato shuddered at the social disintegration creeping in his times. He therefore looked to education to avert this social disintegration. "Education" would become "Social Education" if it averted social disintegration. Instead of this defensive attitude, education may also be so devised as to bring about a positive change in society. John Dewey himself recognises this. For according to him, education may also signify the sum total of processes by which a community or a social group whether small or large aims to secure its growth. To distinguish education used as a means of social change from the use of it as a means of mere maintenance of *status quo,* we may call the former "Social Education." We are not concerned here with the kind of social change for which education can be used as a means. The Americans use Education as a means of Americanisation. The Russians use Education to make society Communistic. If the social change aimed at is approved, the "Education" used as the means is called "Orientation Education" and not "Social Education". If the social change aimed at is not approved, the "Education" used as a means is called "Propaganda Education" or "Regimentating Education" and not "Social Education". In either case there is no need to use "Social Education" in sense 4. Both parties produce literature as a help to the "Education" in view. It is possible to write a book on "Social Education Literature" in this sense. But then it can be called "Orientation Literature" or "Regimentating Literature" as the case may be. However, this book is not concerned with the production of literature of that kind.

Social Education—Sense 5

Thus Social Education is not used in this chapter in the sense got by coupling Education with any of 23 of the 24 meanings of "social". The only meaning of "social" still remaining to be considered. Meaning of "social" is not single but double. For "social" may pertain to the welfare of society in general or it may restrict itself to a class or classes below or likely to fall below the community standard of well-being. If "social" with the first of these meanings is coupled with Education we do not get any new sense for "Social Education". Thus we have to examine "Social Education", only when "social" has the second of the above meanings. This is sense 5. This is the only sense in which "Social Education" is used in this chapter.

"WHAT?" OF SOCIAL EDUCATION

The epithet "social" in "social education" invites attention to the strata of society below the community standard. As shown by the example under meaning of "social" in *the New English dictionary* this use of the term "social" made its appearance only at the turn of the present century. Strictly speaking the example is taken from a passage printed in 1897. The volume of the *New English Dictionary* listing meanings of "social" was published in 1919. This proves that this meaning had not established itself firmly till that year. However, the supplementary volume published in 1933 includes "social service" among the terms defied. The definition given to this term is "service for the betterment of the poor and the like."

History of the Term

In 1912 the American Association of Social Workers appointed a Committee of Terms to define exactly the terms involved in social work. The first concern was with the term Social Work itself. After several attempts, it was found that the only way was to define the term by enumeration, *i.e.*, by a detailed and exhaustive list of each social work activity actually current at the time. The list went on swelling so that this definition by enumeration failed to satisfy the primary canon of definition, *viz.*, that it should be short and potential. In 1928 the First International Congress of Social Workers which met at Paris took a step forward by reducing the long list of social service activities to four major groups—

(1) Cure and prevention of physical disorder or injury or disease and supply of amenities to those who have physical handicaps;

(2) Treatment and relief of the criminals and the supply of amenities to the criminals under treatment;

(3) Relief and prevention of poverty and supply of amenities to those who have economic handicaps; and

(4) Removal of conditions which hinder progress in economic life, and aids to personality adjustment.

For brevity we may refer to these four fields of social service as—

(1) Physical handicap;

(2) Mental handicap;

(3) Economic handicap; and

(4) Personality handicap.

This effort of the first international conference went a long way to clear the ground. The term "Social Service" began to denote something definite. The 1924 edition of *Webster's Dictionary* gave the meaning to "social".

Definition

Social education then is the process of bringing up to an accepted standard the social groups below the community standard in regard to their education or personality development. This work has no doubt to be done by lifting up each individual. And yet the main objective is the lifting up of the group. The work does incidentally give education to individuals. And yet, the main objective is to do something lasting and enduring for the future of the group served, in regard to education.

Normal Sector Covered

The above definition has obvious implications about the extent of the community to be covered by social education. Normally it cannot exceed 50%. This 50% will always be there. Because 50% of the community will always be below the average of the community. Persons in this group are generally slow to mature. They have also economic handicaps preventing the prolonging of their school-going age. They have often to leave school without getting the full benefit of school education or gaining capacity to educate themselves further without the guidance of teachers. Because their family wants them to work and earn. Agencies of social education therefore keep open house for them to enter. A few years of active life with the family or in a craft add to their maturity. At this stage, they enter the portals of social education agencies. They may draw benefits from them during out of work hours, while still in work. On the other hand, provision may exist for their withdrawing themselves temporarily from work and entering the portals of social education agencies. The latter happens in Denmark. Their well-known social education agencies are called Folk High Schools.

Abnormal Sector Covered

In communities without provision for universal compulsory elementary education, even superior men fail to get opportunity for education while in school-going age. They grow up as illiterates. With this handicap, their education is arrested. Before the middle of the nineteenth century, many persons above the average in their mental capacity and personality used to remain illiterate in most countries. But during the last one century, countries in the phase of robust activity and expansion have removed this ugly phenomenon. Hardly any person above the average in his mental capacity and personality comes within the purview of social education. But no country in the phase of cultural exhaustion had been able to set this matter right. In such countries social education has to care also for men who are above the community average in all respects other than education and capacity for self-education, with the aid of recorded thought.

India

India belongs to the latter class of countries. It has been in a state of stupor and political subservience during the period of the spread of universal compulsory education. It has now recovered from its stupor. It is now wide awake. A new life pulsates. A new awareness has come. It has an ambition to come up to world-standard as quickly as possible. Its vast percentage of uneducated folk is a handicap. The percentage is as high as 85. Surely 85% of the nation cannot be below the average in their mental capacity or economic competence. The social education of India today has therefore to care for two groups—the abnormal and the normal ones. The abnormal group comprises men and women of superior personality—superior to the average. 35% of the nation belongs to this group. The normal group is there awaiting social education as in any other country however well-developed. This factor should be borne in mind in the designing and production of Social Education Literature in the India of today.

Content

The content of social education may be described as common sense knowledge and a knowledge of the scale of values current in the community. Common sense knowledge includes a set of non-specialised information about physical materials, plants, animals, language, religion, economic processes, customs, persons and groups. It is knowledge which every individual should possess in order to perform the role of a member in his community. The scale of value concerns the foundation of the existing social order. It usually centers round some religious morals, political or economical set up. A knowledge of vocabulary and grammar underlies the rules of verbal communication. Popular religious knowledge is bound up with rites and abstentions to be observed in the regular course of life. Rudiments of economic knowledge are implied in the distribution and consumption of goods and service. Elements of psychological and sociological knowledge underlie the norms involved in social relations, personal roles, group organisations, civic responsibility and the constitutional set up of the country. Education does not cover vocational knowledge in great detail. But it may include the knowledge of the rudiments of the basic sciences throwing light on vocational practices.

"WHY?" OF SOCIAL EDUCATION

In former years adult education was used to denote the educational effort of the community to help the classes below community level. The political necessity to exercise vote at the polling station was often the motive for adult education. Correspondingly the dominant objective of adult education was literacy. But several modern developments in the social sphere have helped the emergence of social education of a more extensive kind.

Rights of the Democracy

The first is the recognition of the right to education—development of personality to its own fullness, at its own speed and in its own way—right to education, of the democracy or the lower strata of society. These are not intellectuals. They are sure to be immature. They are economically handicapped. According to democracy, these handicaps cannot deny to anybody the right to education.

Implications of Democracy

The second development in the social sphere, helping the emergence of social education is democracy in the political sense of the word. The democratic form of State is being evolved or established everywhere. One of the assumptions of democracy is that sovereignty is inherent in the people. It is presumed to be evenly distributed among all of them. For practical reasons the sovereignty of each may be exercised only once in a few years. The form of its exercise is usually the vote cast at the poll. The result of the vote is the delegation of the sovereignty to a preferred few. One implication of this democratic type of political organisation is that Mr. Everybody—even among those below the community level—should be an informed person. He has, therefore, to be helped with correct information. This cannot be done by party machinery as it will be biased. There should therefore be a public project to help him in the matter and to keep him fit to receive help.

Population Pressure

The third development in the social sphere is the increase in population pressure. It has reached a measure which makes the voluntary bounty of nature inadequate to the vital need of humanity. At first the particular regions of the earth, where the pressure shot up beyond the capacity of nature's bounty, managed to get relief by sending out the excess population to areas of low pressure. By this and other means pressure was distributed. When over-pressure again developed in certain regions, the people of that region acting under the urge of that pressure exploited the sluggish people in low-pressure regions and partially transferred to themselves the gifts of nature in those regions. This colonial exploitation needed better informed personnel in large numbers. It also needed the industrialisation of the exploiting nation. Industrialisation replaced handicraft by Machino-facture. Machino-facture needed men with precise knowledge. The increase of its efficiency needed constant sharpening at the level of the fundamental sciences and the absorption of the results of this sharpening by a wide circle of persons. Changes in process were made from time to time and the success of their working depended on the re-education of the adults employed. Re-education had largely to be through self-education. To maintain the individuals below the average of the community in a mood of curiosity to know and in a state of competence to learn, social education is necessary. Today the population pressure has crossed the limit in several of the undeveloped countries also. The vital needs of food, clothing and shelter etc. have, therefore, to be met only by scientific methods of making nature yield more, and of creating, out of raw materials unfit for direct consumption, fabricated man-made materials fit for consumption. This again needs better-informed persons than hitherto. More of them are wanted than hitherto. More changes have to be made more frequently in the processes than hitherto. The ordinary worker taking part in the arts and crafts has to be kept mentally more alert and resilient. This makes social education a necessity.

Social Maladies

Whenever population pressure increases beyond a measure, not only disequilibrium sets in between people and vital needs like food, but disturbances arise also in social relation. Since population pressure has now gone beyond measure in several countries, a very injurious emotional relation gets generated between national groups. Whether of individuals or of social groups, emotional disturbances have a tendency to persist in the mental plane for a long, long time even after the causal disturbances in the vital plane had died out. The mind of man and the mind of nations have to be helped to throw off such emotional after-effects. One method of effecting this is to set up social education centres to feed the mind with correct information and inducing in it a better sense of values through the supply of comparative views. Social education has the responsibility to promote amity not only within the nation but also with other nations.

World Content

Humanity has now to work for its vital, mental, and spiritual sufficiency in a world-trend, which had long ago transcended the closed systems of village life and of provincial or regional life and is struggling to replace even closed national systems by a world-system. However much national barriers persist in matters material, they have been nearly washed out in matters mental. Occurrences, utterances and additions to knowledge of all kinds in any corner of the world get reported in print and relayed everywhere. All thinking has now to be in a world-context of facts and figures. It is necessary to keep the members below the community level curious to acquaint themselves with the world-context. It is equally necessary for the social education centres to give them the information needed to satisfy that curiosity.

Leisure

Definition

Another happening in the social sphere which is demanding Social Education is the demand for a new way of using leisure. The dictionary defines leisure as "Period or spell of free or unoccupied time." Leisure is not however, strictly unoccupied time. There can be no such time. Verse 22 of Chapter 18 of the *Gita* says that no one with a vital body can fully give up action of any kind.

Remember again the rapturous utterance of Saint Tayumanavar: "It is impossible to have any moment of life unoccupied". Leisure must be occupied. It may be occupied fruitfully or it may be mis-spent licentiously. Unharnessed leisure will wreck us and eat us away. Many are the dangers of unorganised, uncontrolled and unoccupied leisure. There are many demons ready to seize it and through it seize us also and ruin us. One such demon is idle gossip, the very degeneration of the art of conversation. "The soul is dyed the colour of its leisure thoughts" said Dean Inge. "How to live on twenty-four hours a day" has been the theme of a book written by Arnold Bennett.

State and Leisure

Arrangement and enjoyment of leisure is an art which needs careful thought and preparation. The art of life, indeed, consists largely in the capacity to spend wisely and happily the moments in which we are most free—free form the demands and behests of others, free from the demands of relaxation and hygiene, free to plan our activities in and at our own time. To waste these moments is to waste something extraordinarily precious. One of the most horrible and insensate forms of cruelty is killing time.

It is a most vital concern for organised society—the State—that the leisure of its citizens shall be wisely spent. Change the character of a nation's leisure and a corresponding change in its efficiency and culture is bound to follow.

Margin of Leisure

It may be put in another way. We often speak of the Margin of Leisure. As a librarian this reminds me of the wide and narrow margin of a piece of writing on the page of a book. Often, alas, there is little or no margin in which to write in books produced by machines under the paper-controller's injunctions. But when the margin is wide, what do we do with it? Sometimes when the print is fine and the matter is irreproachable, the margin is left white and clean save for a few remarks for personal appreciation and corroboration. Sometimes as in the exercise-books that we have to read, the margin must be filled with corrections in blue pencil and red-ink. We have to do similarly if the text of the printed books is faulty, one-sided or poor. So when the daily text of life is poor and mean, the margin of leisure must be to correct and re-adjust it.

But the ideal is symbolised by the illuminated books of the Middle Ages that belong to the days before the age of the machine. The big black letters of the small space of text are surrounded by beautiful and delicate pictures and decorations brightly coloured scrolls and leaves and flowers or landscapes and portraits that illustrate and illuminate the text. And in Utopia, and Rama Rajya as we would call it, the margin of leisure will be wide and full of beauty, if indeed the text and the margin are distinguishable; a man's leisure will illuminate and illustrate his work. For work and play, industry and art, will have come together; leisure will complete the life of work; and work will complete the life of leisure. Till then we must prize the margin of leisure vouchsafed for the masses, however small. We should help them to fill it in an organic way. Thus education for leisure and the enrichment of adult life is no light educational activity; it is no peripheral problem; nor is it an incidental task. It is rather a fundamental problem, affecting the welfare of society and its prosperity. As such, it should receive major consideration.

Out-Moded Utilisation

Free time means time not required for doing certain necessary things, demanded by bodily relaxation and hygiene or economic or spiritual needs., A very efficient mode of utilising leisure which centuries of folkways had stabilised has now been rendered unavailable. This outmoded utilisation was of the group variety. As those were days of mass illiteracy, the leisure was transformed by some folk-institutions into periods of intellectual, social and spiritual enrichment without dependence on literacy. The holy-days were days of religious, social and family festivals. They did not connote days of inaction. They were filled in an organic way. As the whole community had leisure at the same time, it was spent in the rewinding of the individuals and the community as a pleasurable group-project.

Such modes of using leisure are dying out with the impact of industrialisation and urbanisation. Another efficient and stable way of utilising leisure has to be evolved. Western countries in which this phase began about a century ago have been experimenting in various ways. India, which is entering this phase only in the present generation, can put their experience to use and shorten her own period of transition.

New Mode

The new mode of utilising leisure which the West is stabilising is through Library Service. It has realised that the mere putting in justaposition of the books of the library and the people during leisure time, does not lead to the occupation of leisure by reading for realisation or inspiration or information. The affinity between books and men is weak. It is particularly so in the case of men below community standard. Social Education is the means by which this affinity has to be strengthened.

"HOW?" OF SOCIAL EDUCATION

All the methods mentioned need to be adapted to the needs of Social Education. In adapting them, there is one point to be borne in mind. During the state of illiteracy, people had been depending on group-activity for utilisation of leisure. Such people are more community-minded than individualistic in their ways and outlook. This indicates that the methods of Social Education for the newly literate should learn more upon group activities like film-shows, exhibitions, talks, reading circles, discussions, and carrying out of community projects.

LIBRARY

Sweden

The spontaneous organisation of reading circles, with a small library as the nucleus, among the labourers of Sweden during the last ten years, acts as a pointer. No less than 20,000 such reading circles have come into being in this short interval. At first most of these nuclear libraries were found in social education centres in industrial areas. During my visit to Sweden in 1948, I gathered from the National Labour Union that the agricultural community too had begun to ask for small libraries of this kind. The practice in Sweden is for the State to give either the money or the books—subject to a maximum—asked for by any social education centre. The books become the property of the Centre. However, most of the centres pass the books on to other centres, after they have finished reading them. In these social education centres we find the maximum possible activation of a small but purposive collection of books.

Great Britain

In Great Britain too the place of books in social education had been equally improved. The Library of the University of London has, for example, got a section for supplying books to centres of tutorial work. These correspond to social education centres. The leader of the centre gives a list of the books required. He mentions also the number of copies required of each book. The University Library procures these copies, by purchase or by inter-library loan, and sends them to the centre. The centre keeps the books as long as required. They are usually kept on often for six months after a particular course is over. Thereafter the surviving books are returned to the University Library for circulation to other centres. When I visited London in 1948, I found as many as 40,000 books in store for serving social education centres. Again, the present National Central Library of Great Britain started as Central Library for Students. This Library was formed just for the purpose of supplying books to Workers' Educational Associations in different localities.

Special Importance of Libraries

People below community-level cannot absorb information or understand a problem or argument by hearing only once. This is true even of people above community level. One has to come back to it again and again to refresh one's memory. It is on account of this that lecture method or any other method is not by itself sufficient. Access to books is necessary. At the same time access to books is not by itself sufficient for people below community level. They should be prepared by the social education centres to look for the books and use them. Their curiosity should be roused by the methods of discussion, dramatisation, project, etc. in vogue in the social education centre. It is only thereafter that there will be a chance for people to come back to books again and again to refresh their memory. Eventually this habit of going to books may even induce in them a certain urge and capacity to educate themselves ultimately with the aid of books and without dependence upon help by a regular teacher. This indicates the great dependence of social education on suitable books acceptable to the members taking social education.

India

But such books do not exist in India today. We have to think out what books we want, who should write them, how they should be built, who should find the theme for the books, and who should organise the whole work. This is the crucial problem in Social Education Literature today. It is on this problem that this book is turned.

MESSAGE OF THE GITA

The *Gita* gives an analysis of the nature of personality as a whole and of the intellect and of the will in particular. It enumerates groups. This occurs in Chapter 8 verses 26 to 35. This analysis may prove helpful in distinguishing the role of social education from that of higher education.

Sattvic Type

Sattvic Personality

(1) is free from attachment;
(2) does not speak about himself;
(3) has will;
(4) has perseverance; and
(5) is unchanged by success or failure in achieving.

Sattvic Intellect can distinguish between,

(1) action and inaction;
(2) what is to be done and what is not to be done;
(3) fear and fearlessness
(4) bondage and liberation.

Sattvic Will controls, through unswerving concentration, action of

(1) mind;
(2) life;
(3) breath; and
(4) sensory organs.

Rajasic Type

Rajasic Personality

(1) is emotional;
(2) seeks fruits of action;
(3) is covetous;
(4) is given to violence;
(5) is impure; and
(6) subjects himself to pleasure and grief.

Rajasic Intellect does not care to observe true distinction between

(1) propriety and impropriety, and
(2) what is essential to do and what is not.

Rajasic Will

(1) pursues virtue; and
(2) runs after pleasure and holds on to wealth, by force of attachment and motivated by expecttion of fruits.

Tamasic Type

Tamasic Personality

(1) has no anchorage;
(2) is primitive;
(3) is inert;
(4) is wicked;
(5) acts indiscretely;
(6) is indolent;

(7) is dejected; and
(8) procrastinates.

Tamasic Intellect

(1) is shrouded in darkness;
(2) mistakes impropriety for propriety; and
(3) understands everything in a perverted way.

Tamasic Will is in a state of delusion and indulges in

(1) sleep;
(2) fear;
(3) grief;
(4) dejection; and
(5) conceipt.

Types of Nations

Generally speaking no person is purely *Sattvic* or *Rajasic* or *Tamasic*. Every personality will be a mixture of these three types. But for all practical purposes, a personality dominantly Sattvic is taken to be virtually Sattvic. So also a personality dominantly Rajasic is taken to be virtually Rajasic. Similarly a personality dominantly Tamasic is taken to be virtually Tamasic. In a nation or any other natural group, there will be a certain proportion of these three types of personality at any one time. The quality of the nation is determined by this proportion. Its success among nations will also be determined by this. Its internal life will be characterised by this proportion. Indeed a measure of its culture will be this proportion. Its efficiency will also be determined by this proportion. Corresponding to the dominance of one or other type of personality in this proportion, nations themselves may be regarded as Sattvic, Rajasic and Tamasic, respectively. Tamasic, Rajasic and Sattvic dominance are in order of evolution. Each nation endeavours to progress up this line of evolution.

School-Going Age

The progression of a personality along this line of evolution is his development—his education. The continuous action of social environment from the birth of a person pushes his personality either up or down this line of progression. Sankara has therefore emphasised a dominance of Sattvic personalities in the environment of a person to be a factor in pushing him up instead of down the line of progression. Indeed he has prescribed *Satsanga* (=Association with sattvic persons) as the potent factor in eduction. In the school-going age, the teachers form a dominant part of the social environment of a child. Education of the child is therefore made or marred by the type of teacher employed. To draw them from the Tamasic group is fatal. To draw them from Rajasic group is no doubt better. However, it is not the best. The proper thing to do is to provide Sattvic personalities as teachers.

Adulthood

In the education of the adult, dependence on teacher has necessarily to be less than in the case of the education of the child. There are three reasons for this. Firstly, due to economic factors, the adult has no leisure to spend sufficient time in the immediate presence of a teacher. Secondly, the adult is more egotistic than the child; therefore he will not be able to stand a teacher's presence for as long as a child. Thirdly, a nation may not be able to spare a sufficient number of Sattvic personalities to provide teachers for all the adults; moreover the field of interest of an adult is much narrower than that of a child; a person with the same field of interest alone can be efficient in teaching him. The chance to find a Sattvic teacher specialising in the same particular field of interest as the adult, is even smaller than that of finding any Sattvic teacher, whatever. Therefore the adult has to depend for his education largely on association with literature. But a Tamasic person would find it difficult to draw all the necessary help from literature alone. The nation should therefore spare some Sattvic people to act as triggers in the education of such adults. With their encouragement, guidance and the influence of their presence, these adults can educate themselves through literature.

Self-Educability

In studying the relation of reading materials to Adult Education, we shall have the occasion to make use of the concept of self-educability. In a sense, it is a vital concept. Much will therefore be gained by devoting a few lies to this concept. In so doing, we shall mention and explain a few statistical terms. The use of these terms will make communication briefer and more exact.

Dependent Education

Education implies attainment of certain skills in the use of the primary senses and the movement and use of the body and the limbs, appreciation and observance of a certain scale of values, adoption of and adaptation to a way of life, enriching one's memory with a certain amount of information, sublimating the emotions, sharpening the intellect and strengthening the will. In the very early stage of life, certain movements are the result of mere bio-chemical forces. Other movements and skill are largely learnt by imitation. Even the filling up of memory with language elements and the development of the intellect are dependent largely on imitation. Scale of values and way of life are picked up by observing the other members in the family and the surrounding community under social pressure. Thus much of early education depends on the immediate presence of persons who are fit for profitable imitation. It often happens that the rate of education gets accelerated if another person gives a helping hand, underlies points, and administers repetition-practice. The presence of such a guide or teacher makes one's education dependant and formal to that extent.

Definition

But after this stage, some people develop capacity to move forward in their education on their own steam without dependence upon the immediate and constant presence and help of a teacher. No doubt he will draw help informally from every element in his environment. Only this environment will not have a formal teacher. This is well emphasised in an episode in the *Bhagavata*. While walking through a forest, Shri Krishna meets an effulgent, care-free, genial man. He asks that man: "You are so happy. You look so wise. Who was your teacher?" The other person replies: "My teacher! The sky, the earth, the birds, the wasps, the stars, the mountains, the rivers and the donkeys, this very forest, my friends, my relatives and indeed everything which I come across." But he did not mention a formal school or a formal teacher. A person like that is said to educate himself. His self-educability is of a high order. In those days there were no printed books. Today printed books will be counted among the various elements in the environment, which help self-education. We may then define self-educability as the capacity to educate oneself, with the aid of books and the other elements in our environment, but without depending on formal teaching.

Scale of Self-Educability

It will be a help if we can postulate a scale of self-educability. At one end of this scale, we shall have persons who do not at all want the help of a teacher. The measure of their self-educability may be taken as 100. At the other end of the scale, we shall have persons who lean upon teachers for everything. The measure of their self-educability may be taken to be zero.

Quartiles

Let us imagine all the persons of a community arranged in descending order of self-educability. The first 25% of the community are said to constitute the "first or the top-most quartile" in the skill of self-educability. Similarly the second 25% are said to belong to the "second quartile." The third 25% constitute the "third quartile." The last 25% are said to belong to the "fourth or the last quartile." The second and the third quartiles are sometimes together mentioned as "The Middle Quartiles". Similarly the first two quartiles are together mentioned as "The Upper Quartiles" and the third and the fourth quartiles are together mentioned as "The Lower Quartiles".

Centiles

Instead of taking groups of 25% of the total community, we may also take groups of one per cent of the total community. Each such group is called a "Centile". We can also speak of the "top-most centiles" and the "bottom-most centiles".

Deciles

Similarly, by taking groups of 10%, we get a "decile".

Adult Education

The term Adult Education is usually applied to the education of the two lower quartiles of the adult population of a community. The presumption is that the adults in these two quartiles depend on the help of teachers for their further education. On the other hand the adults of the first two quartiles can manage their further education through self-education.

Gita Categories

To use the *Gita* terminology, the Tamasic type is generally made of the last quartile and the lower third of the third quartile.

The Rajasic type coves the rest of the third quartile and most of the second quartile. It may even occasionally extend into the first quartile. In a developed community, the Rajasic type may not be so large. The Sattvic and the Rajasic type may be more or less equal in extent. This is only a rough indication. The nature of the literature suited to the self-education of a person is bound to vary with his position in the scale of self-educability. We shall go into this in the next section.

Literature

National Education Literature

The educational policy of a nation should be to bring each of is members to full development and to place on a harmonious basis his relation with the other members and the material environment. The literature required for it may be called National Education Literature. The nature of the literature required for the education of an adult depends upon his place in the line of evolution form Tamasic to Sattvic personality. But Literature is seldom produced to meet the exact needs of an individual adult. It can only be produced for the nation as a whole. However, the same type of literature will not be suitable to the education of all the three types of personality in the nation. Some differentiation has to be made. Broadly speaking, three types of literature may be recognised. Each type may be named after the education intended to be aided by it. In fact, education itself is of three types.

Research Literature

Sattvic education would put the Sattvic type of persons in pursuit of things-in-themselves—that is research on the highest order. The firm will of the Sattvic persons, their unfailing perseverance, their detachment from any fruit of action, their unswerving concentration and their highly organised personality will warrant literature being produced for them in a highly organised, condensed and solid style, on the most advanced subjects, and in a supreme key. This may be called Sattvic Education Literature or Research Literature. This book is not concerned with its production.

Higher Education Literature

The education aiming to lift the level of the Rajasic group of the nation towards the Sattvic may be called Rajasic or Higher Education. Higher Education should help the Rajasic group to see the unity, and the reconciliation, hidden behind apparent diversity and conflict. The will of Rajasic persons to pursue anything capable of producing the desired results, and the need to help them discriminate between propriety and impropriety and between what is essential to do and what is not essential, to have their emotions sublimated, to have their covetousness extinguished and to abstain from violence and to purify themselves, warrant literature being produced for them in a lucid and moderate style on diverse subjects and in an elevating key. This may be called Higher Education Literature.

Social Education Literature

The education aiming to lift the level of the Tamasic group of the nation towards the Rajasic may be called Tamasic or Social Education. Social Education should help the Tamasic group to escape their beguilement by petty, irrational and unsubstantial interests, to activate themselves in bigger and substantial issues affecting their own life and their community, and to participate in the national endeavour to raise its level of life. The literature for the Tamasic group should be endowed with qualities capable of lifting up their spirit, pulling up their cheer and dissolving their darkness. It should enable them to distinguish what is proper from what is improper. It should rescue them from their proneness to wickedness. It should melt their inertia. It should chasten their awareness and discretion. It should shake off their dejection. It should develop concentration in them. And it should induce agility and quick action in them. For this purpose, it should centre round subjects affecting their daily life. It should further be in a simple style. It should have pictorial and other aids. This class of literature may be called Social Education Literature.

11

Social Education Literature

The word "Literature" in the title of this book should first be defined. It is not used here in the restricted sense of "writings whose value lies in beauty of form or emotional effect." Neither is it used in the sense of "writings of a country of period." Nor is it used in the sense of "the books treating of a subject." For the purpose of this book and in the way in which it is used by the organisations devoted to the promotion of Social Education, "Social Education Literature" does not mean either poems, dramas and stories whose theme is Social Education, or monographs, textbooks and treatises on Social Education. It means merely "printed reading and kindred materials suited to the needs of persons undergoing Social Education." No doubt the use of the term "Literature" in the sense of "printed material" is rather colloquial. But in this particular combination, it has been lifted to the level of Standard English. To put it short, "Literature" is used here in the sense of "book"—the universe of books. The epithet 'Social Education' merely restricts the attention to a sector of this universe. Our first business should therefore be to define that sector. There are various approaches to this problem. The universe of books can be dissected in various ways—(1) by standard, (2) by utility, (3) by value, (4) by nature of embodiment and so on. We shall pursue the problem along each of these lines.

STANDARDS ANALYSIS

We shall first group books by standard. In this we have a helpful Vedic tradition. When I was struggling with this problem in 1939, Swami Turianandа Brahmendra Saraswathi, disciple of Swami Svayamprakasa Brahmendra Saraswathi of Sendamangalam, happened to call on me. He mentioned four standards of exposition recognised in Indian tradition *viz., Prabhu sammita* (=Seminal literature), *Suhrith sammita* (=Research literature), *Kanta sammitha* (=Expository literature) and *Sisu sammita* (=Elementary literature). This Vedic analysis put me on a helpful track.

Seminal Literature

Seminal literature is fundamental. It emanates from "seers". Seers work more through intuition than through intellection. No doubt they bring what they "intuit" unmediated by intellect or primary senses, to the level of intellectual communication. The seers are self-centres of illumination. They are few and far between. Their occasional advent is still shrouded in mystery. Seminal literature fertilises several minds in the upper-most centiles (in the intellectual scale). It appeals to them only. It affords a tool for application in the furtherance of thought.

Example—Sir C.V. Raman's paper entitled *A new radiation* (1928) which appeared in the *Indian journal of physics* is Seminal Material. Another universally known example is Darwin's first contribution on *Origin of species.* The account of Foci, Facet, and Phase in *Library classification: Fundamentals and procedure* has perhaps some claim to this class.

Our definition of Social Education makes it obvious that Social Education Literature is not concerned with seminal literature.

Research Literature

Research Literature is advanced literature. It embodies the results of investigation in specialised fields. It is produced by whole-timed or part-timed research-workers. It is intended for circulation among peers and co-workers in the field. It facilitates team-work. It helps avoidance of turning intellectual energy over regions already fully cultivated.

Example— The hundreds of papers listed in the *Indian journal of physics* (1930–1932) under the title *Bibliography of Raman Effect* consist mostly of Research-Contributions. So are the thousands of papers on evolution and other related problems, which have appeared in biological periodicals since Darwin's days. Many of the papers appearing in the *Annals* of the Indian Library Association belong to this class.

Our definition of Social Education makes it obvious that Social Education Literature is not concerned with Research Literature.

Expository Literature

Expository Literature is rich in flair. It is personal in its method. It displays much judgement in the selection of details. Its style is racy. Once we begin to read it, we are led from page to page. We do not like to be disturbed. It has an aroma of its own. It is alluring. Our curiosity never wanes. It even grows. We want to finish it at the very sitting—even though is takes us late in the night. Turning its pages is like turning pages of life itself. It is illuminating. It is such books that make reading popular.

Example—Raman's own account of the Raman Effect forming his Nobel Lecture or his contribution to the *Malaviya commemoration volume* is an Expository Contribution. The delightful talks on Raman Effect which the Madras audience was accustomed to hear from Prof. J. P. Manickkam is also a contribution of that kind. So are the various papers that Huxley wrote in defence of Darwinism and the popular expositions of relativity by Eddington and Jeans. Some of the articles in the *Granthalaya* of the Indian Library Association are of this class.

Our definition of Social Education makes it obvious that Social Education Literature is most concerned with Expository Literature. It is only books with flair that can appeal to the lower intellectual strata. They should therefore come within the purview of Social Education Literature.

Elementary Literature

Elementary Literature is elementary in language, style and thought. It is suited to the lower quartiles in the intellectual scale. Those in lower quartiles are slow to mature. They are seldom able to reach a high standard. This does not mean that they should be allowed to stay put where they are. Their levels should be lifted however little it may be. At any rate they should be prevented from being enveloped or being dragged deeper into ignorance. Much of this will have to be done by person-to-person aid. But even here it is possible to take the aid of books in follow-up work. They can be, only if they are elementary. To suit neo-literates, the language used must be nearest to the spoken word. To suit the lowest intellectual quartiles, the style should be simple. Sentences should be short. Figures of speech must be concrete. Allusions should be to folk-lore rather than to erudite classics, In the thought plane, each book should cover only a small area of any subject. Even there, deeper levels should not be touched. Books should be descriptive and factual. Sojourns into abstractions should be avoided. And yet elementary literature does not mean children's literature. Though adults in the lowest quartile and children are both intellectually undeveloped, there is a vast difference between them. There is mental rigidity in the adults; and yet in some respects it would have reached a greater maturity. Overlooking this vital difference, children's books are sometimes prescribed for the adults learning in Social Education Centres. Such books wound the sense of pride in the adults, though it be in the unconscious mind. The adult therefore seeks to withdraw himself with revulsion. It is therefore necessary to write elementary books specially turned on the lower intellectual quartiles among adults.

Examples—Early in the nineteenth century a few souls in the British community, who became sensitive to the call of Social Education, braved the ridicule of die-hards and established the Society for the Diffusion of Useful Knowledge. This Society published many elementary books in several series. One series was finally cumulated and made into the *Penny cyclopaedia*. Another series was entitled *Gallery of portraits*. The *Pictorial bible* is another surviving monument of the missionary zeal with which this Society provided Elementary Literature in the thirties of the last century.

Our definition of Social Education makes it obvious that Social Education Literature is concerned with Elementary Literature even more than with Expository Literature.

News Literature

Outside the Vedic analysis, modern society has evolved a new class of literature which may be called News Literature. Its main objective is to give current facts. Occasionally it brings back to public memory facts of the past which had gone out of mind but which might be of current interest. It also prefixes or suffixes, to the core of news, some extra-actual narrative on topics of current interest. Going round the Social Education Centres of the Delhi Municipal Committee, one is impressed by the great hunger, which the neo-literates and the lowest intellectual quartile have for News Literature. This is evidenced by the large crowd of people who stand before the wall-newspapers scanning them word by word. Though the scanning is slow, the absorption is remarkably intense. It looks as if nothing can pull them away in those moments. This experience shows that there is need for a species of News Literature, quite different from the ordinary newspaper, but suited to the needs of Social Education.

Standards for Social Education Literature

Thus we see that generally speaking, Seminal Literature and Research Literature do not come within the category of Social Education Literature. Elementary Literature of the adult variety should form the core. This can be re-inforced by a specially designed variety of News Literature. These will be the main kind of literature needed by neo-literates. Social Education Literature can also include Expository Literature. Various grades are possible in this species to match the various removes of the adults from the state of neo-literacy and to match also the various levels of their mental maturity.

APPEAL ANALYSIS

The word "literature," in its setting in the term "Social Education Literature", denotes printed material. Printed material is characterised by severe abstraction. It represents thought. It is indeed intangible thought transformed into tangible and portable something. Thought is so transformed to facilitate communication. When communication is from person to person in each other's immediate presence the spoken word is supplemented by every element in the environment. The most vital and the richest element is the personality of the one who communities. The modulation of the voice, the movement of the limbs, the changes in the face, the subtle movement of the eyes and indeed the total personality, combine with words in making the communication effective and unerring. In printed literature, all these aids are totally absent. It is the cold undifferentiated string of words alone, that is visible. A sound film or a gramophone plate too abstracts the voice. But the abstraction made by printed literature is of a further remove. For what is to be sensed or what is visible is only a black-and-white pattern on paper. The primary symbol is not a meaningful picture in the pattern but only a phonetic symbol. It is only a group of them that becomes a meaningful symbol. The abstraction and the analysis have thus been carried to a much greater extent in printed literature. It has therefore to depend upon appeals of various kinds to be accepted by a reader. We shall therefore examine the possible appeals of printed literature.

Intellectual Appeal

Most of the printed literature is dominant in its appeal to the intellect; and the transition from what is visible on paper to the impression it produces on the intellect is virtually instantaneous. Reading will be comfortable only if it is so. This happens only in the case of those who can find interest in thought of various degrees of abstraction. Abstraction is greatest in the sciences—physical, natural and social.

Our definition of Social Education makes it obvious that Social Education Literature cannot include any large quantity of literature in these subjects which are essentially abstractions. It is only the expository form unusually rich in flair that can annex Pure Sciences to Social Education Literature. Even in the most developed countries, social Education Literature does not include much material of such intellectual appeal.

Emotional Appeal

Emotional appeal is within the reach of many more, than intellectual appeal. There is perhaps some physiological reason behind this. The subtilty of emotional appreciation increases however with intellectual development.

The range of emotional appeal is vast. Literature is possible and exists to suit the entire range. There are passion stories at one extreme. They are characterised by the depiction of gross mountainous waves of passion. These make an easy appeal to the lower intellectual strata who form the subject of Social Education. At the other extreme we have delicate, almost unexpressed and imperceptible, humour suggested in a most oblique manner. This trace-emotion makes an instantaneous appeal only to the gifted few. Considerable reaction-time with help from guides may make some others perceive and enjoy it. But our definition of Social Education makes it obvious that Social Education Literature cannot include materials lying in the latter half of the above mentioned emotional range.

Sense Appeal

We said in the last section that the emotional apparatus is more widely developed than the intellectual one. It can be easily seen that the sense-apparatus—primary senses—is even more widely developed. It is fairly well developed even in the lower intellectual strata. This means that concrete entities are more easily recognised and an account of them more easily understood, than conceptual entities and an account of them. This fact should be fully exploited in Social Education. To this end Social Education Literature should be rich in description of concrete things and situations. It should press into service plenty of illustrations which directly make impressions on mind, without undue dependence on the medium of words. The illustration will have to be in the form of pictures—life like pictures and not schematic diagrams—in the literature intended for the lowest intellectual strata. For slightly higher strata the illustration can be a combination of pictures and a graphic description in words, particularly of movements, in equal measure. For still higher strata, abstract schematic diagrams may replace life-like pictures and effect some economy in words. For the highest intellectual strata, illustrations may be a comfort but not a necessity. Confinement to concrete things and situations is neither necessary nor sufficient.

Experiential Appeal

For the highest intellectual strata, literature is the hunting ground for adventure. The more removed the theme developed or the thing described is from experience, the greater its appeal is. This gap between appeal and experience goes on diminishing as we go down the intellectual strata. When we reach the lower quartiles, that are the subject of Social Education, it is only that literature which is closest to experience, that is accepted. Social Education Literature should therefore centre round the actual experience of the class of readers for whom it is intended. At the same time, if it does not cross the boundary of experience, it will serve no educational purpose. While its solid core should be what is within the experience of the readers, it must extent its fringe beyond that core. The extent of this fringe will have to vary with the degree of intellectual development of the diverse strata of readers. This means that the range of experiential appeal of Social

Education Literature will have to be very varied indeed. It is the proportion of the fringe to the core which appeals to a given stratum of readers. If this proportion is too great, the literature will have no meaning to some, and will therefore stand unnoticed. If the proportion of the fringe to the core is too small, the literature will be too incipid and will therefore stand rejected by others. This subject has not yet been properly investigated anywhere. It looks as if it has not even been recognised. Common people are usually condemned as incapable of reading books. This is locating the snake in the wrong bush. The snake is not in the reader. It is in the literature. This must be recognised. This must be set right.

Utility Appeal

Experiential appeal is followed in its wake by utility appeal. Experience has roots in the past. Utility has some forward roots in the future. Experience induces interest and a fringe of curiosity to have a peep just beyond experience. Utility stimulates interest and curiosity even more powerfully. The economic pressure in modern life increases the potency of utility appeal. Literature, which will enable a worker to do his job better and thereby earn more, will certainly be accepted willingly. It may even be sought voluntarily. At any rate, it will need far less of pursuation for acceptance.

An incident which comes to mind will illustrate this. There was a person who made his living by fruit-gardening. His produce had to be sent by rail to a distant market. He used to send them every week. It happened that in certain week the parcel office rejected his packets. The fruits perished and he lost heavily. He had been all along a problem to the district librarian. He would not accept book service. He ridiculed reading books. He refused to receive the librarian in his house lest he should be persuaded to read! The librarian had been biding his time. Hie missionary zeal had made him sense the predicament of the gardener, which was brought about by a change in the specification for packing fruits to be sent by rail, of which he remained ignorant by his refusal to read. The librarian therefore sent him a copy of the latest booklet on the subject, issued by the Board of Trade. Lest he should smell the library and refuse the book packet, he suppressed all mention of the source. The gardener read it. He packed his fruits in the new way. The packet was accepted. He was delighted. A fortnight later a letter went from the librarian asking the gardener to return the book as it was overdue. The gardener wrote that it was too good a book to be given away. He had never realised that it came from the library. Probably he thought that it came like manna from heaven! The librarian promised to send even more books on packing and, what was better, even books on improving his gardening work. In the end the librarian was invited to dinner. Before going, he ascertained from the gardener whether the hairy quadruped which once chased him out of his compound would allow him to enter his house! The gardener not only became himself a convert to reading; but he also became a proselytiser!!

Social Education Literature must exploit this utility appeal. This implies that there should be literature on every conceivable art and craft. People of the lower intellectual strata making their living in particular crafts can be made to take to literature only if we start feeding them with literature on their own respective crafts and gradually take them to other pastures.

Prestige Appeal

Not infrequently the position accorded by a given society to different kinds of literature determines their appeal. This is prestige-appeal. Hierarchies of prestige once established and lived in, are apt to survive changing conditions. They often defy rational explanation. In the context of social forces, prestige is shifted consciously or unconsciously from one class of literature to another. Prestige-appeal is dominant in the higher social strata. Its lure makes some sincere souls spend mid-night oil. It turns cleverer people into frauds. These often pick up the names of new literature at one club table, overhear remarks on it, fly away like predatory birds, and build up their prestige in other clubs by a pretentious parade of their knowledge of the literature. The prestige-appeal diminishes as we go down the social strata. But it never vanishes completely. Even the lowest quartile—in the social as well as the intellectual scale—do respond to prestige appeal at least to a slight degree.

Perhaps there is nothing objectionable in Social Education exploiting this prestige-appeal of literature. In a sense this prestige-appeal of literature may degenerate to the same level as the gossip-appeal of conversation. So long as one is on guard against such degeneracy, the acceptance of Social Education Literature by the folk concerned may be facilitated by investing it with some element of prestige-appeal.

Integration of Appeals

The most successful Social Education Literature should integrate all the six appeals in due proportion. By varying their proportion, Social Education Literature can be attuned to the responsive capacity of the varying intellectual, occupational and social strata. If a society has literature with all grades of integrated appeal, Social Education can, with comfort, take the people from one grade to another by gradual steps determined by the capacity, the interest and the speed of development of each individual.

VALUE ANALYSIS

The value of literature can vary widely. Its range can be infinite. At one extreme, it may elevate and inspire. At the other, it may depress and corrupt. It may sublimate personality or dissipate it. It may humanise or de-humanise. It may entertain or inform. This wide range of values can have full play in literature falling within the area of the Humanities and the Social Sciences. It may not be altogether absent even in the literature falling within the area of the Natural and Physical Sciences.

Spiritual Value

Literature of global value exists. It is often found in the realm of the sacred books of religion. But the originals of sacred books are often too vast to be read or mastered by the lower intellectual strata. We therefore often have a class of Social Education Literature culled out of sacred books. In conformity to the proneness of the lower intellectual strata to respond better to sense-appeal and experiential-appeal, these anthologies are made predominantly of anecdotes, episodes, parables and dramatic situations. Stories from the *Upanishads,* the *Purans,* the *Jathake tales,* the *Talmud,* the *Bible* and the *Koran,* are often brought out. These are often bereft of religious creeds which are bound to change from time to time. On the other hand they consist mostly of spiritual experiences of eternal value. These stories have often a reach beyond the restricted religious practices of the religion from whose sacred books they are extracted. Indeed they are all alike. They all speak in the same voice. The closer they are to what is eternal, abiding and fundamental, the greater is their spiritual value as Social Education Literature.

Message Value

Just short of sacred books and yet as near to the centre and as eternal like them, there are several classics in literature. The *Ramayana* is a supreme example of this class. Consequently there is no end to the number of the versions, adaptations and renderings of the *Ramayana*. The value of this class of literature is the ever-lasting message it carries with it. The simplicity of their language and the economy of their art are unmistakable. The ring of the message which they carry is equally unmistakable. The first few chapters of the *Ramayana* give a poetic picture of the very depths of human experience from which such literature with message blossoms forth. Valmiki claims that such a work will last and endure so long as the mountains and rivers endure. Goethe has explained it in one of his conversations. He says that when a poet dives into his own depths, picks out his pristine experience and recedes from the depths towards the level of consciousness, he feels the urge to express his experience for the benefit of humanity. He is obliged to use the language current in his community. He irradiates it so profoundly that its glow is extremely rich in colour. It carries with it diverse messages. Apart from poems we have also, in modern times, collections of sayings of great souls like the *Sayings of Sri Ramakrishna*. They too are of the same order. They too are carriers of message.

These are all too profound to be absorbed by anybody, in a reading or two. People of the upper quartiles read them over and over again. Each one picks up only that message which the valve of his own experience allows. All the other messages are screened off for the time being. Books with a message are often too powerful and too dazzling for most men. Therefore this valve-mask of his experience is a help. He ruminates over the particular message he has picked up. He partially integrates it into his own experience. He grows. His experience grows. He reads it over again. He is now able to pick up another message. The cycle is repeated. The same old words of Valmiki have communicated to me progressively varying messages. This is one way of using literature with message value.

But these epics and poems and sayings are usually too vast for the men of the lower quartiles. We have therefore slices of them, which have a concrete anecdotal flavour, reproduced for their benefit. Sometimes it may be mere scissors-work. But if it is re-told by a contemporary creative author with sympathy for the lower quartiles of his community, the effect is even greater. Literature with message should be relayed to the common man in this manner. Social Education Literature should seek enrichment of this kind.

Mirror Value

Any good work of literature—using literature in the restricted sense of poetry, drama, fiction and essays—is a mirror of life. So it is with biography as it has developed in recent years. Some years ago P. Jaganathan, wrote a short story in our popular Tamil weekly *Ananda vikatan.* It was entitled *Milk-man.* One day after its appearance, our milk-man came to us with great glee and was proud that he had been written upon. When somebody pointed out a sentence in the story, he burst out with a laughter of supreme complacence, "Yes, Sir. It is true that all of us milk-man do mix water with milk, though our young author has put it jocularly as mixing milk with water!" He wrote another short story entitled *Aunt.* Almost every lady in our neighbourhood claimed that it was a picture of her own self. Shakespeare has used this mirror-value of literature in the play within play in his *Hamlet.* The ups and downs of the characters give vicarious satisfaction to the reader. He sees his own ups and downs mirrored in them. The entertainment value of such mirrors of life is unbounded.

Vicarious Living

According to a school of literary criticism, literature has the high social function of purging persons of their passions and other frailties by helping them to live them out vicariously in the characters created by the artist. The effectiveness of this mirror-value depends on the ability of the poet to invest characters with passions and frailties and to depict them in such a way that it weans the audience away rather than make them imitate the characters in those very passions and frailties. The tenth book of the *Bhagavata* is a supreme example of the success of the poet in raising this mirror-value to the highest level. Hardly any poet in any language known to me has reached this level of success. But all worthwhile literature does have this value in some measure. If society does not have such first rate poets, at least adaptations of ancient classics to modern conditions of life should be stimulated.

Drama

Poetic form of literature is often beyond the comprehension of the lower intellectual quartiles who form the subject of Social Education. The same may be said about literary essays also. Dramatic form is not so difficult and yet not quite easy to comprehend. This is because the words in dramatic literature pre-suppose being supplemented by histrionic art. Men in the lower intellectual quartiles cannot supply this supplement from imagination. The value of dramatic literature in Social Education is in its use in preparing for witnessing a performance with intelligent appreciation. It may also happen that it is enjoyed with greater ease, if read after the performance is witnessed. The great zeal with which neo-literates turn to dramatisation suggests that dramatic literature should form a good part of Social Education Literature The colour with which the drama is dyed may range through the entire field of knowledge. Religion, Psychology, History and Social Criticism can form the theme. In the theme for drama, representation should be given to all such interests. Not long-drawn-out plays but one-act plays should be selected. One-act plays lend themselves for amateur performance as leisure-time occupation after the day's work. Those whose day's work is repetitive get their total personality blossom forth by such activities. In organised communities, one-act lays can be easily popularised. All that has been said about dramas is equally applicable to sound-picture.

Fiction

Fiction is the form of literture that produces the most effective mirror-value on the lower intellectual quartiles. Yarn-spinning and story-telling have been the oldest pre-occupation of man and the earliest attraction of children. It has been the chief method of filing up leisure-time as well as the means of relief from boredom. It still remains so. The colour with which fiction is dyed may range through the entire spectrum of knowledge. Even science, relativity and fourth dimension have formed subjects of entertainment. Religion has always been a theme. Psychology, love and crime characterise the most widely sought fiction. Historical personalities as well as common man's life give life to another class of fiction. Long-drawn-out ponderous novels do not fit with Social Education Literature. It is short stories that are suitable. The short stories will appeal to anybody on account of their rapid movement and the narrowness of their canvass. Such stories are particularly suited to neo-literates. Before the strain, caused in the exercising of newly acquired literacy, begins to over-power emotional interest, the story will be rounded off, if it is a short one. Even abstract subjects can be concretised by this method.

Addiction Complex—A possible danger in the fiction that looms large in Social Education Literature is that the criminal and other undesirable events portrayed are not handled in such a way as to have a chastening effect but so as to make the undiscriminating and unsophisticated people to imitate. Fiction of that kind is likely to produce "addiction" complex. The chief problem in the Social Education Literature of this class is to portray life in such a way that it helps us to escape from the common place without taste being vulgarised or "addiction" complex being induced.

Biography

Biography, including auto-biography, is only second to fiction in its general appeal. The hero of physical prowess has always been the centre of attention and his life-story has therefore a personal appeal. In modern times the hero of physical prowess has begun to share his place in popular imagination with heroes in other fields. Men of eminence, industrial magnates, persistent explorers, great educators, penterating psychologists, discoverers in biology, inventors of machinery, chemists, physicists and even mathematicians make an appeal to the common man. Such biographies are also written in modern times with considerable literary insight. To read the adventures of heroes in any field gives vicarious satisfaction. The thrill of vicarious satisfaction can be as real as that of personal satisfaction. The reader of a biography comes to realise that every difficulty or handicap can be overcome by the unconquerable mind of man. The life of Charles Darwin convinces a cripple that physical weakness need not be an obstruction to his development. Life of Justice T. Muthuswamy Iyer induces the feeling that poverty need not be a barrier to his advancement. Biographies of this kind provide at once entertainment and the solace that the spirit can dominate the material conductions of life.

Fictional Element—In modern days a biography, in which the author tells in his own words his subject's thought as in Strachey's *Queen Victoria,* appeals even more than ordinary biography. Use of the fictional element, handled with restraint and judgement, is dowering biography more and more with the charm of fiction. Social Education Literature should be made rich by this form of biography.

Biographical Fiction

It is almost impossible to differentiate between biography which employs the technique of fiction and biographical or historical fiction proper. Their border-lines are merging in modern times. Their mirror-value is indeed very great. They form a good component of Social Education Literature.

Information-Value

The fiction and fictionised biography are deeply flavoured with the personality of the author. But the personal flavour helps the acceptance of the literature by the ordinary reader. For it lessens the intellectual effort involved in reading. But those, who are not at the very lowest rung in intellectual scale, prefer putting forth some intellectual effort of their own to know facts as they are. The literture, suited to this class of people or to this mood in readers, consists of travel and history. These describe life in communities and incidentally portray lives of individuals too in a way that is far less personal. This impersonal presentation takes the description nearer to what may be called public description. It is objective, as it is called. In this the reader escapes the influence of the author. This implies that he has to go without the help of the aroma of the author. The result is that he has to lose the help of imagination and lean much more on his intellect. Objective or sense-dependent concreteness implies some abstraction. For it abstracts what is nearer to the grasp of the primary senses and a varying degree of intellectual comprehension, and leaves out what may be subtle and intangible. It is the absence of this intangible element—the trace element—

in the objective accounts of travel and history that makes them appeal to the intellect rather than to imagination and makes reading less attractive. However, the gross wholeness of the situation is not shattered too much. That is why travel and history come next to fiction and biography in their claim for inclusion in Social Education Literature. Travel covers a shorter range of time and is more impressionistic, and less thorough in detail than history. History may cover any range of time and is more objective and detailed than Travel. Moreover there are writings—plenty of them—which belong to the region in which fiction and biography form one side, and travel and history from the other, meet and overlap. Examples of works which are near the factual end of this region are the histories by Froude and Macaulay and travels like the *Eothen* or the *Man eaters of Tsavo*. Works which are near the fiction end of this region are called biographical fiction and historical fiction. *The Edwardians* by Sackville-West and the *Baladitya* by A.S.P. Ayyar are examples.

Travel

Travel books can have all the charm of fiction and all the thrill of biography. Their lightness of touch and concreteness are elusive and yet science, geography, history and anthropology can lie imbedded in travel books. Here again the vicarious satisfaction given by a travel book makes a great appeal. The more brilliant the writer is and the more delicate the fusion of literary merit and penetrating insight is, the greater becomes that satisfaction. There is also a great social service which travel books can do. If they are written in a spirit of tolerance, fair-play and appreciation of the culture and the ways of life of the people visited, they can become a powerful medium for promoting international understanding. Travel should form a good and popular proportion of Social Education Literature.

History

The more chronicling history is, the more abstract it becomes and the less appeal it has to the non-specialist. Social and cultural history is more global and less abstract, and appeals to the common reader. *Outline of history* of H.G. Wells is an example. So is the *Discovery of India* by Jawaharlal Nehru.

History books may appeal only to the higher strata of the lower quartiles. But it must be possible to write history in such a way that it can appeal to all and become a valuable part of Social Education Literature.

Science

There are several informative books in the Physical, Natural and Social Sciences. In fact they are abundant in these subjects. Their informational value is of great importance to the upper quartiles—the intellectuals—who pursue these sciences. But they are too abstract to the lower quartiles. Even a book like Bhaskara's *Leelavathi*—a fictionised book on arithmetic with an unusual flair—is too abstract for inclusion in Social Education Literature.

Integration of Values

In the days when the masses were illiterate, it was the sacred books, the *Puranas* and the epics that used to be expounded to the masses. Even today the masses continue to be illiterate. This institution of exposition of literature is still being continued. We may call this institution "Katha". The exposition is usually done after the day's work, in the early hours of the night. It takes place in front of the village temple. Sometimes it is accompanied by music. The story is often used as a slender thread round which a good deal of religious, philosophical, ethical, historical, economic, social and legal information with topical flavours is dexterously woven. I have seen huge audiences kept spell-bound by "katha". There is no attempt at political indoctrination. The talk is mostly turned on cultural topics. It is all criticism of life bathed in bubbling wit and humour. When I was in Madras recently, I attended two such expositions by Srirangam Satakopachariar. I was deeply impressed by their high social educaiton potential. Illiteracy is no handicap where such an institution for Social Educaiton is kept alive. With literacy, this institution can be taken to a higher level. The audience can be put on to a follow-up study of what they heard in the exposition. It will be another step to allot some of the evenings for a discussion or a debate by the audience. This discussion or debate may well be based on a study of relevant books. Social Educaiton Literature can thus be brought to and integrated with an institution which has been successful for centuries in the promotion of Social Education among literates and illiterates alike. Even in urbanised areas, the masses have brought with them this old village institution of evening exposition. Social Education Literature should be integrated with this institution and its value fully exploited in any organisation officially or unofficially promoted for the furtherance of Social Education.

Value Scale

The following may be taken as the value scale of Social Education Literature:—

(1) Anthologies from sacred books, the epics and other literary pieces, and folk-lore.

(2) Fiction including biographical fiction;

(3) Biography including fictionised biography;

(4) Music and fine arts;

(5) Travel;

(6) History; and

(7) Arts and crafts.

EMBODIMENT ANALYSIS

Literature includes not merely original books of the conventional type but also magazines, folk-fores, reprints of classics, translations from foreign classics, omnibus craft-centred sets and pictures. These embodiments are becoming common now-a-days. The reprints and translations are popular with the upper quartiles. Though, except in the case of folk-lore, they may be a little too advanced for the lowest quartile, they can form a substantial portion of the Social Education Literature intended or the third quartile.

Magazines

Weekly and monthly magazines can be effective media to entertain and inform those who are subjects of Social Education. Such magazines can be made attractive with plenty of illustrations and cartoons. They should begin with an appetising pithy exposition of one or two matters of topical interest. They can contain short stories, and extracts from epics, *Puranas* and sacred literture. They can also contain accounts of foreign countries, and historical and economic information. They may also devote a column to questions and answers. *Ananda vikatan* is an example.

Folk-lore

In the far oft days when society was simple, a village formed a more or less closed unit; intimate neighbourhood-relation prevailed; and community-life was lived in an integral way. Though there was no literacy, the exuberance of contented life often led to creation of folk-songs and folk-stories. These have been taking shape through several centuries. These were transmitted from generation to generation by word of mouth. Local festivals within a radius of a few miles, traditions about great poets, reformers and kings, and the vocations of the people had been themes of such folk-songs and folk-stories. Many of them had been composed and set to music to keep time with the rhythm of work. Some of them reflected the spontaneous outburst of joy in the simple folks of those days at the harvest season and at the spring. Some embody myths and legends about local rivers and hillocks as well as national rivers like the Ganga, Yamuna, Sindhu, Godavari, Krishna and Cauvery, and national mountains like the Himalayas and the Vindhyas. Some of these folk-songs are folk versions of the great epics. They are simple and transparent. They scintillate rustic fun and wit. They have the power to throw the common folk into a care-free mood of enjoyment. When they emerge from this mood, they find themselves elevated and fresh. One of the useful things which agencies responsible for Social Education can do is to bring such folk-songs and folk-stories to print. If it is done their standards will be just suited to Social Education Literature. Their appeal and their value will be of the right sort. This section of Social Education Literature will be eminently suited to the lowest intellectual quartile.

Reprints of Classics

We suggested in this chapter that Social Education Literature should be integrated with the traditional, unofficial, village or community institutions called "Katha" for expounding books to a large gathering. We further said that the books, which were expounded in these institutions, were old classics. In the past when the audience were illiterate, the expounding leader of the gathering was the only person who had a copy of the book. I have seen it often to be an old, dilapidated, unattractive copy. Since modern social education should aim at leading people to read books for themselves, it is necessary that there should be reprints of classics—not merely sacred books, puranas and epics, but classics in all subjects. We get a preview of what should happen in this matter within the next generation, by examining the development of the reprint of classics in the English-speaking countries, with which we had been brought into close contact. It is worth dealing at length with this subject as this class of books will have to enrich our Social Education Literature considerably.

Definition of Classics

Let us begin with a definition of classics. Classifier's definition of a classic given in my *Colon classification* is: 'A book which stimulates other books and literature on itself.' The inherent qualities of a classic, which stimulate such auxiliary literature, are:

(1) It has elements of permanent value;

(2) It is saturated with the personality of the author—which in itself was very powerful and highly organised; and

(3) It is a seminal book cutting new ground, blazing new trail, stimulating new thought and so on.

The basic sacred books of a religion are of such a nature. Works of true poets, dramatists, novelists, and other literary artists are more or less of such a nature. But classics are not peculiar to the main classes 'Religion' and 'Literature'. Any other subject may have classics of its own. There are biographies and travel books which have become classics.

Emergence of Reprints

One of the most inspiring developments in the book trade of the English-speaking world is that of the popular reprint. Social Education through cheap reprints of classics came into vogue in the middle of the nineteenth century. Chambers, Cassel and Knight were pioneers in the scheme. Bohn's Libraries, established in 1846 included half a dozen well-known series of reprints of standard English books. As many as 600 volume were brought out. These became common companions of the common men for several generations. Describing their value to Social Education, Emerson said that these reprints did "as much for literature as rail roads have done for internal intercourse". As the reading public steadily enlarged through the nineteenth century, the flow of reprints increased immensely. Everyman's

Library began in 1904. This was followed by the Modern Library in 1909. World's Classics is another popular series. In recent years Penguin books were started in 1935 as a six penny fiction reprint series and got reinforced by the Petican Books devoted to reprints in Arts and Sciences and Pelican Specials in politics and current events. In the first three years 23,000,000 Pelican books were distributed. In 1948 its American Branch was named New American Library of World Literature. The fiction series goes by the name 'Signet Books' and the art and science series by the name 'Mentor Books.' It is said that in one year 184,000,000 copies covering 659 titles were distributed. The secret of this immense mass distribution is said to be the highly organised system of distribution through news-stands, local stores and cross-road centres spread throughout the country to the extent of 60,000 centres.

Translations of Foreign Classics

One of the functions of Social Education is to widen the horizon of interest. Unesco rightly insists that one of the means of promoting world peace is to extend the cultural horizon of the common man far beyond his linguistic boundary. One of the means of doing this is to make accessible to him the classics of foreign literature—literature not produced with any propaganda motive—but the one which blossoms forth spontaneously from the inner-most self of the most sensitive souls in a community. Proficiency in languages other than the mother tongue is almost impossible for the lower quartiles. The only way in which foreign classics can be made accessible to them is through translations. Some of Shakespeare's plays have been so translated into some of the Indian languages. Some of Tolstoy's fiction have been similarly translated. In the present transition period when Indian society has yet to discover its creative authors, an easier alternative may be to enrich Social Education Literature by translations of foreign classics.

A Model

A monumental example of translated classics is "Loeb's Classical Library". The English speaking community owes this to the private philanthrophy of James Loeb. He founded the series of translations going by his name to bring within the reach of the common man "all that is of value and of interest" in Greek and Latin literature from the time of Homer to the fall of

Constantinople. Each volume gives in parallel pages the original text and the English translation. The series began in 1912, and it produced a hundred volumes by 1919. It is estimated that the number may extend to about 500. Begun and continued till 1934 by G. P. Putnam's Sons, it has now gone to the care of the Harvard University Press.

International Interest

In 1932 the International Institute of Intellectual Co-operation started a quarterly index to current translations under the title *Index translationum.* The war led to its suspension in January 1940. Its successor-body Unesco has now resumed the *Index translationum.* The 1950 volume published in 1952 lists 13,516 translations published in 34 countries classified according to their subject-matter and gives three different indexes for authors, translators and publishers. Unesco goes even a step forward in the matter of translations. It aids in the selection of materials which deserve to be translated. It also takes an active interest in improving the quality of translations.

Omnibus Craft-Centered Literature

In section 225 reference was made to utility appeal. So also in section, 224 the importance of experiential appeal was stressed. The masses of our country have been so much accustomed to be treated to the puranas, the epics and philosophical and spiritual literature, that literature often means nothing else for them. The modern economic pressure is turning their mind more intensively to their own arts and crafts. They find that the traditional methods of work are beginning to crumble. They feel the onslaught on their vocation by market-disturbances on a world scale. These factors loosen their fixations. They are almost thrown into a mood of anxiety and a sense of uncertainty. It will be a mockery to the masses in that predicament if the conventional Social Education Literature is forced on them in the conventional way. We have to experiment on another approach. It should call it the "approach of interest". The psychology of interest indicates production of what of I call "Omnibus Craft-Centered Literature". There should be one such set for each of the commoner crafts.

The volumes in a set will fall into three major groups: (1) Vocational, (2) Informational, and (3) Cultural.

General Description

The vocational group will have three sub-groups: (1) Primary Craft, (2) Subsidiary Crafts, and (3) Background of Fundamental Sciences. The books on the latter two must be focussed on and radiate from that of the primary craft.

The informational group will consist of volumes which start with what is immediate in the daily life of the vocational group and then progressively extend to remote factors. Whatever be the vocational core, the informational volumes will ultimately tie up with materials on economics, co-operation, local self-government, extended functions of the government of a modern State, the political structure of our Republic, the change which is coming over the distribution of wealth, and the dependence of the welfare of the nation on each citizen playing his part.

The cultural group of volumes should relate the vocation which was the starting point with the fundamental and eternal literary sources through anthologies and books specially written for the purpose. These should provide opportunity for the people to appreciate and enjoy forms of literature and other kinds of Fine Arts like Music, Dance, Painting and Graphic Arts. It is possible for some of the cultural group of books to be shared in common by the omnibus literature centering round diverse crafts.

An Example

As an example, I give below a tentative chain of subjects which should be covered by an omnibus set of volumes centered round potter's craft:—

(1) Pottery
(2) Pottery decoration
(3) Brick-laying and Tilemaking
(4) Doll-Making
(5) Clay-its physics and chemistry
(6) Descriptive geometry
(7) Mensuration
(8) Commercial Arithmetic
(9) Pot as a percussion instrument
(10) Ceramic industry today
(11) Ceramic geography today
(12) History of pottery in diverse lands
(13) Pottery in chronology and ethnology
(14) Folk songs on pottery
(15) Folk tales on pottery
(16) Spiritual lyrics centered round pottery

I am giving here some examples of cores for such craft-centered literature:—Basket making, Weaving, Dyeing, Metal-work, Wood-work, Embroidery. Lace-making, Toy-making, Home economics, House decoration, Farming, Plant life, Animal husbandry, Animal life and so on. The omnibus set of volumes centering round the craft of paper making, which was brought out in England some years ago, will show the way. Since the general level of education and of modernisation of craft-methods is of a much lower order in India today, due modification must be made in following this model.

Sound Books

A new embodiment which is coming into vogue in Social Education Literature is what is known as 'Sound Book'. It consists of a book printed in bold type and a set of gramophone plates inserted in its pocket. These plates contain a reading of the book. The Department of Education of the Columbia University is making considerable observations and experiments in the service of such books to neo-literates—children as well as adults—and the lowest intellectual quartile. Public libraries provide a special room where such people can play the gramophone records and follow the book with the eyes as well as ears. This class of books has great potentiality in making books acceptable to the lowest intellectual quartiles of all standards of literacy, and to the neo-literates in all quartiles. Perhaps the use of such books will hasten the process of learning to read. Sound-recording instruments are now becoming fairly cheap. It must be possible for such books being produced in all subjects in which the people coming under Social Education are likely to be interested.

Pictorial Literature

Another form of books which should figure considerably in Social Education Literature is the one which consists mostly of pictures. The *Picture Ramayana* for example is well-known. The *Das Indien*—a book of pictures—published in Germany became very popular even with the university students, when a copy of it arrived in the Madras University Library about 25 years ago. A picture appeals to the primary sense of sight. It makes a direct appeal through the eye with a minimum of intellectual effort. The more direct and less symbolic the picture is, the more helpful it will be as Social Education Literature. For symbolic pictures require an interpretation before their meaning is sensed by the intellect. As symbols, the letters in a printed book are even more removed from direct apprehension. For, a letter represents not an idea but a unit sound or phoneme. It is only a set of consecutive letters, which form a word, that has a meaning. Even then the meaning it gets in association with other words is often different. In fact a complete meaning is not only by taking whole sentence or a set of sentences together. All this means a hurdle which is far too much for the lower intellectual quartiles. Even people in the uppermost quartile instinctively prefer a pictorial representation to a verbal description, if both the alternatives are available to them. This is perhaps a consequence of the fact that ever since humanity had the power of sight it had been apprehending forms and figures directly. Apprehension mediated by phonetic symbols is a recent introduction in the history of humanity. Seeing is therefore a more dominant and more preferred method of picking up communication than reading.

Visual Literature

In recent years, we hear much of visual aids. These have their prototype in "shadow plays" and "puppet shows". These were media for communication to a crowd, even as the "Katha". The medium of plays and shows was pictorial and that of Katha was verbal. Katha which is a medium for picking up communication by a crowd in public is now being partly replaced by printed literature which is a medium for picking up communication by individuals in privacy. So also shadow plays and puppet shows which were media for picking up communication by a crowd in public can be replaced by "Visual Literature" for picking up communication by individuals in privacy. However the term "visual aid" is still being restricted to what is absorbed by a crowd in public. The only difference is that technology is used in the production of these aids and we call them cinema shows or silent-pictures. But there is no need for this restriction. Visual aid can be adapted for use by individuals in privacy. Pictorial literature is what we will get by such an adaptation of visual aids for individual use. With histograms, graphs, cartoons and other forms of picture, any theme can be communicated through visual literature. The pictorial literature may be embodied in book form or may also be in the form of film strips, even as reading material is nowadays thrown into the form of film strips.

Audio-Visual Literature

In the talkie or sound-film, technology has provided a medium by which communication can be picked up by a crowd in public simultaneously through the eye and the ear. This is called "Audio-Visual Aid". It should be quite possible to adapt Audio-Visual Aid also to individual use in privacy. Just like the sound-books, it is possible to have Sound-cum-Picture Books or Audio-Visual Literature as a form of Social Education Literature. This has not yet been attempted. But whereever a large mass of illiterate population is to be helped by Social Education Organisations, this new form of literature will be of immense use. It is true that as things are today, the cost of production of such books will be very great. But it is upto the technologists to work for reduction in the cost of production. The cost per copy can also be reduced by producing this material in sufficiently large quantity. Even then, this kind of audio-visual literature may not come within the means of the lower intellectual quartiles as they are also often lower economic quartiles. The only means of getting over this difficulty is to provide copies of such books in public libraries and lend them for free use as a public project, even as ordinary printed books and gramophone records are being lent. This proposal will require considerable planning and organisation on the part of the State to make it economically possible.

Universal Use

There is one factor which may bring Visual Literature, if not Audio-Visual Literature, within economic possibility. For pictorial literature transcends the limitations of language. Their language is, so to speak, universal. It will therefore be possible to produce pictorial literature on a much larger scale than books in particular languages. This means that the current extra cost of printing pictures can be nearly extinguished by increasing the number of copies in the edition. Almost any theme—be it for entertainment, information or inspiration,—will lend itself to communication through Visual Literature. There is plenty of artistic capacity running to waste in the country. It can very well be harnessed. If it is done, Social Education Literature will become popular and effective with the lower quartiles. When Society finds wisdom in producing braille books for the physical blind, there is no reason why it should not produce visual books for the mentally purblind who are not able to stand the strain of reading printed words.

EXTERNALISED MEMORY

During the last two hundred years, a new species of books has come into being. These are Reference Books. We all understand what is meant by a Reference Book. But it is rather difficult to give a exact definition. An obvious definition is the functional one—a reference book is one that is looked up for specific information of narrow extent. The inadequacy of this definition to define reference books in a sharp manner can be realised if we remember that not infrequently one goes to compendious treatises for such information. For example when specific information about the date of opening of the Pamban Bridge was sought, the only book from where it could be picked up turned out to be Dudley Stamp's *Indian Empire.* A negative definition is: A reference book is one which does not lend itself to continuous reading. This definition brings in not a little of the personal factor of the reader. As extreme cases mention may be made of individuals for whom even dictionaries are fit forms for continuous reading. In mediaeval India, dictionaries and indexes were learnt by heart with the implication that they were read and recited continuously. The classic in dictionary, the *Amara kosa* is a well-known example. This linguistic dictionary was composed in metrical form to facilitate being read continuously and memorised. Perhaps the best way to avoid such involuntary lapses into inconsistencies of this kind is to define reference books not by function but in terms of the internal (as opposed to the physical) structure of the book. The peculiarity in the internal structure of a reference book is that it is not made up of continuous writing or exposition. We don't have sentences woven into paragraphs, paragraphs swelling into chapters, and chapters mounting up into the whole book, in continuous pursuit of a single idea, simple or complex. On the other hand a reference book is an ensemble of disjointed entries of short, though varying lengths, the order of the entries being often decided not strictly by thought-sequence but by the accident of the alphabet.

In the case of reference books intended for the upper quartiles they may consist mostly or entirely of formulae, schematic diagrams, statistics, figures, enumeration of titles of books, etc.

But the reference books, which can form part of Social Education Literature, can be only Atlases, Biographical dictionaries and Who's whos, Linguistic dictionaries, Encyclopaedias, Gazetteers and Year-books and Directories.

Value

The chief value of reference books lies in the relief they give to the load of memory. They not only take the place of memory but also extend it to a dimension which would have been impossible but for their invention. Man wants information almost at every moment. Even the common man wants it. When society was simpler it was enough for him to get the information by direct observation and enquiry then and there. In this, the primary senses proved sufficient. But he soon outgrew this stage. He was often in need of old information—too old for the primary sense to help him. This led to his developing a new faculty—memory. Soon a man with a capacious memory gained in popular estimate. Again man wanted information about themes and occurrences at far off places which were too distant for his primary senses to overcome. Then he had necessarily to depend upon the memory of others who had been in those far off places and enriched their memory with the aid of their primary senses. Dependence on such individuals was rather precarious. To meet this situation, demand arose gradually for a new type of books which would furnish information readily. It was soon realised that the more bereft such books were of rhetoric, the better they served the purposes. I call such books "Externalised Memory".

Advent

This new class of books was late in coming. About three centuries lapsed since the invention of printing before a few books of this class began to appear here and there. It took still another century before they grew to a respectable number and their class got christened as "Reference Books". The *New English Dictionary* has been able to trace the name only as far back as 1836. This reference is to the article on the 'British Museum' in the *Penny cyclopaedia,* V_5, p. 455, which has the following sentence: "Dictionaries and lexicons in languages, with more than 8,000 books of reference, are constantly open for the use of students of the reading-room in the cases and presses which surround them." The first recorded use of this term in the writing of a professional librarian is in the *Memoirs on libraries* (1859) of Edward Edwards the doyen of British librarianship: "What are in a special sense termed books of reference such as Collections, encyclopaedias, Lexicons, Dictionaries, etc." (V2, p. 634). In the English-speaking world the first encyclopaedia appeared in the middle of the eighteenth century. The first linguistic dictionary also belongs to that period. The earliest known directories are J. Brown's *Directory or list of principal trades in London* (1732); and Whitehead's *Newcastle directory* (1778). Two of the earliest informational yearbooks are *The yearbook of facts in science and art* (1827) and *Congregation yearbook* (1864). These are now defunct. The now familiar *Statesman's yearbook* was founded in 1864 and Whitaker's *Almanack* made its first appearance in 1861. India too has established some reference books during the last few decades. But they are far too few. Developed countries are rich in reference books. In 1938, for example, Great Britain had as many as 2,500 reference books in print. It is estimated that about 1.7% of the books available for sale at first-hand in Great Britain during 1938 consisted of reference books.

Delay

But most of these reference books are of an advanced nature. No country has produced a sufficient number of reference books which can be included in Social Education Literature. As already stated, it took three countries for Reference Books to emerge, after books came to be printed suited to the level of the upper quartiles. It is not even a century since ordinary books came to be produced suited to the level of the lower intellectual quartiles. Therefore it is no wonder that reference books suited to their level have not yet come much into vogue. Apart from this parallelism, probably the urge for reference books will never become as great among the lower quartiles as among the upper ones. This is only a conjecture based on the fact that the curiosity for specific facts is not as high among the lower quartiles as in the upper ones. The result may be that it may not be commercially worthwhile to produce reference books in a sufficiently lower key to make them fit to be included among Social Education Literature.

Hand-Book for Social Education Leaders

This, however, does not mean that there is no demand for ready-reference information from the lower quartiles. Those who act as leaders in Social Education Centres often feel embarrassed by the questions about facts put by adults. In developed countries which have public libraries within easy reach and rich in reference books, the leaders can easily cope with the situation. But in a country like India which has not yet established a public library system, the position of the leaders of Social Education Centres becomes difficult. They have no libraries to go to. Even if there are, they are very poor in reference books. Fifteen years ago the Madras Library Association sensed this difficulty of teachers in adult schools and organised a hand-book in Tamil with about 50 chapters on 50 different topics, each extending to about four or five pages. Due to the disturbance caused by the Second World War the project could be completed only in 1951. It is entitled *Muthiavan virundu* (=Feast for adults) on 38 subjects by 35 authors.

A Scheme

In the light of this experience, the Indian Adult Education Association made an attempt in 1949 to bring out a similar social education handbook of facts in the English language in the hope that it can be reproduced in each of the Indian languages. This attempt however did not succeed, partly because of the fading of enthusiasm on the part of participants to do the hard work necessary to collect up-to-date data on diverse subjects and also because of there being no prospect of finance being found for publishing the book. I am giving here the list of 75 subjects which the Committee on the problem drew up for inclusion in the proposed hand-book:

Part 1 Home Science—Child Care

(11) Care of expectant mother

(12) Child welfare

(13) Child personality

(14) Infectious diseases

(15) Family doctor

(16) Local herbals

(17) Food and nutrition

Part 2 Home Science—Animal and Plant Care

(21) Care of domestic animals
(22) Veterinary information
(23) Dairying
(24) Poultry
(25) Soil and manure
(26) Crop diseases
(27) Farming implements
(28) Kitchen garden
(29) Fruit care

Part 3 Home Science—Clothes and Equipment

(31) Family tailoring
(32) Knitting, embroidery and needle work
(33) Laundry work
(34) Soap making
(35) House decoration
(36) Household electricity
(37) Radio equipment and its utilisation
(38) Household scraps and their utilisation

Part 4 Community Life

(41) Village sanitation
(42) Urban sanitation
(43) Village organisation
(44) Municipal organisation
(45) Co-operatives in village economy
(46) Co-operatives, distribution and supply in urban life
(47) Community living
(48) Bharat-Sevak-Samaj

Part 5 National Life

(51) Indian constitution
(52) Citizenship
(53) Administrative organisation

(54) Transport
(55) Commerce
(56) Communications
(57) Industry
(58) Trade unions and employers' organisations
(59.1) Public finance
(59.2) Education
(59.3) Five Year Plan
(59.4) Culture
(59.5) Anthropological types

Part 6 World Community

(61) India's neighbours
(62) India and the world
(63) India's foreign trade
(64) Indians abroad
(65) The Commonwealth
(66) United Nations
(67) Unesco and other specialised agencies of UN

Part 7 Everyday Natural Science

(71) Look at the sky
(72) Indian calendar
(73) Physics
(74) Chemistry in everyday life
(75) Hydro-electric schemes
(76) Life
(77) Physiology
(78) Hygiene

Part 8 Everyday Social Science

(81) Psychology
(82) Library service
(83) Educational system
(84) Physical geography

(85) Meteorology

(86) Indian geography and geography of the world

(87) Indian history

(88) Legal rights

(88.1) Legal status

(88.2) Property

(88.3) Contractual relations

(88.4) Torts

(88.5) Crime

(88.6) Regulative laws

(88.7) Legal procedure and administration

As a transitory measure, a handbook of this nature will serve as a substitute for reference books at the level of Social Education Literature.

HISTORY

The first books to be printed after the invention of printing form moveable metallic types were the sacred books and other books of religious import. Though other subjects came to be provided for in due course, for a long time they were of a severe standard. They were of the learned variety. They were suited only to the upper-most intellectual quartile. That was but in keeping with the intellectual aristocracy of those days. Even the story books which came to be printed, say in the eighteenth century, were voluminuous—running to several volumes. Their style and language were also too high-flown to be of use to the lower intellectual quartiles. This was still more so in books on positive sciences including social sciences. There was hardly any book on arts and crafts. Arts and crafts practised by the lower intellectual quartiles were mostly learnt by the method of apprenticeship, by direct observation and imitation. Books seldom came into the picture. It must also be remembered that many of the artisans were illiterate.

Dawn

The dawn of Social Education Literature did not set in, even in what are now developed countries, till about a century ago. It took as late as 1851 for the Mechanics' Institute of Great Britain to find as many as 1,000 books as an aid to teaching or for follow-up work. Lord Brougham, who was closely associated with Dr. Birkbeck in adult education, had already promoted a Society for the Diffusion of Useful Knowledge. It found that books written for university men—for the upper intellectual strata of society—were not easily intelligible to the lower strata. To distribute books of such high standard among those, who were below average, amounted to a mockery. It was felt that books should be specially written for the artisans and workers with less of abstraction, everything cohering about concrete situations within their experience—in a word, in a style and form palatable and assimilable to them. The writing and printing of cheap instructive literature was therefore taken on hand. Several tracts were published. The claim of Society to enduring fame, however, rests upon the *Penny Magazine,* the mental food of millions of working-class adults. "Striking points of natural history, accounts of the great work of art in sculpture and description of such antiquities as possess historical interest" filled its weekly issues. The Editorial Board recorded that there had "never been a single sentence to inflame a vicious appetite, no excitement for the lovers of the marvellous, no tattle or abuse for the gratification of a diseased taste or personality, and above all no party politics". While current thought was thus retailed to the workmen, universal knowledge was written down to their level in the *Penny cyclopaedia* which was published in instalments costing a penny each. It extended eventually to 15,000 pages and it was sold to the extent of 75,000 copies. I was able to procure a set of this encyclopaedia for the Madras University Library. Between 1832 and 1834, the Society published the Gallery of Portraits in which biographies of statesmen, warriors and men of science, letters and arts appeared for the instruction and entertainment of the common folk. There was also the *Pictorial Bible* and several other books. This is a measure of the correlation of literature and social education for the masses about a century ago in Great Britain.

Present Day

The development of Social Education Literature in Great Britain, during the presentx century, is also typical. A most extensive organisation for social service to the masses through education is the WEA (=Workers' Educational Association). It was founded in 1903. Its objects are:

(1) To stimulate and to satisfy the demand of working men and women for education; and

(2) To work for a national system of education which shall provide adults full opportunities for complete individual social development.

For this purpose it works in close co-operation with universities and Local Education Authorities.

The WEA owes its origin to Albert Mansbridge, who was a clerk in the Co-operative Wholesale Society. He is now a knight. I met him in London in 1924. I still remember vividly the impress of vision and will on his face. He is one of those who have the intention to locate the root of a matter however hidden and far removed it may be. And so Mansbridge and his co-workers realised almost immediately that the first essential condition for the success of social education was that adults should have constant access to books. In the early days, an *ad hoc* collection had to be made and distributed to the adults as their needs became known. Even in urban centres where a public library existed, it was found in those early years that the books which it provided were not often suitable for the class of adults in question. The limited means available made the *ad hoc* purchase and distribution unsatisfactory. The variety of subjects taught was growing rapidly and the need for a completely equipped adults' library was increasingly felt. A representative cross-section of the book-world was needed. A limited supply hampered the grading of books according to the stage reached by the adults. With the continued growth in the size and variety of the adult student body, some new method was necessary to displace the inadequate and uneconomical system by which each of a number of different bodies tried to meet its own needs. It was to meet this situation that the Central Library for Students was founded in 1916. When I visited it in 1924, it had already grown to great dimensions. In 1931, it was incorporated by Royal Charter as National Central Library and its purpose was extended.

Future

Although there are now many books in most developed countries specially written to build up Social Education Literature, they are all of the ordinary kind with perhaps more of illustrations than for the upper quartiles. These are suited roughly to the third intellectual quartile. The needs of the lowest intellectual quartile have not yet been properly understood or provided for. The delay in their being recognised is partly due to the demand for literature thinning out almost to a vanishing point when we enter and go down the lowest intellectual quartile. Moreover the State has not yet in any country, except perhaps in Russia, taken up full responsibility for every kind of social service and particularly for the provision of Social Education Literature for the lowest intellectual quartile. The production of literature of this sort can never become economically self-supporting. There are various reasons for it. The class of literature has to be largely made of pictures and in the form of sound-books and visual literature and audio-visual literature. These are costly to produce. Even if their cost is brought down, the urge to buy such books will be almost absent in the lowest intellectual quartile for which it is intended. Further even if there is that urge, this folk will not have the wherewithal to buy the literature, since they form also the lowest economic quartile. Thus demand cannot stimulate supply of Social Education Literature of this kind. In fact supply will have to stand severed from demand, and proceed, not under the pressure of demand, but under the pressure of State policy. The little awareness which is coming over the State of some of the socially minded communities about the duty of the State to the lowest intellectual quartile not only on grounds of philanthropy but on grounds of the welfare of the community as a whole, gets easily quenched by the modern mass methods of communication like the radio. The educational profession alone can convince the State that the mass method is the least suited for the education of the lower quartiles, however effective it may be in mobilising their emotion and regimentalising them into an unthinking crowd led by demagogues. Although it is more than half a century since John Dewey proved the futility of the mass method of education and initiated the movement of individual instruction, it has not yet been adopted even for the education of the average people. Virtually nobody has yet begun to think of the ways in which the Dewey-postulate of education can be implemented for the lowest intellectual quartile. It is the same old danger still persisting. We seldom think of people below ourselves, either in intellectual or economic capacity. We simply lose sight of them in all our plans—even in plans specifically intended for their exclusive benefit! We forget the old dictum of

Aesop that what is play to children may prove to be death to the frogs. As the State recognises its duty to the democracy—to the lowest men in democracy—this old habit of ours should change. We should step out of our ivory tower and shape all matters relating to the lowest quartile—including Social Education Literature—in terms of their own requirements and capacities. This is the direction of democracy in regard to the shaping of Social Education Literature in future.

INDIA

One of the chief difficulties, which stands in the way of the successful functioning of Social Education Centres in India today, is the aweful absence of Social Education Literature. Indeed this factor reduces any talk of Social Education work to an academic exercise if not to a mere mockery. To make it real, one has to begin at the far end of working for the production and distribution of Social Education Literature of the right sort satisfying all the requirements laid down in this chapter.

Book Famine

The present book-famine in the sphere of Social Education is due to historical causes. Before India went into sleep during the present cultural cycle, printing had not been discovered. People lived in small, virtually closed, village communities. Life in a village was fully integrated. Village life itself was education enough to answer the needs of the times. Nature's bounty was plentiful. It was more than sufficient to maintain the population which then existed. Therefore the content of Social Education was mostly concerned with matters of religious, philosophical and spiritual import. These matters do not change as quickly and as continuously as matters concerning the physical and the natural sciences. India did not wake up till a few years ago. It was during this period of long sleep, that printing was invented, and democracy established itself, and population pressure overturned nature's capacity to provide food, shelter and clothing without the help of technology and scientific methods of agriculture. Though India began to head towards a crisis in this matter of balance between population pressure and nature's unsolicited gift, her political subjection and state of cultural exhaustion prevented India falling in line with the other countries. The rulers were not interested in Social Education.

Wherever education people had was along the traditional lines of Kathas, shadow-plays and puppet-shows. There was no attempt at universal literacy and compulsory education of children. Not even 15% were literate. Without literacy, there can be no question of development of Social Education Literature.

Future

But today India has shaken off her sleep. It has recovered from her exhaustion. Mahatma Gandhi has secured political freedom. This has given India freedom to manage here affairs in her own interest. The first thing that the States in India have to do is to care for Social Education. When they set about arranging for Social Education, the famine of Social Education Literature stares in its face. Lifting this famine would involve overcoming five groups of difficulties which may be labelled as: (1) Language, (2) Experiential background, (3) Illustrations, (4) Publishing, and (5) Marketing. Of these the first two lie in the sphere of the author who is the producer of the thought embodied in literature, and the last two in the sphere of the business world which is concerned with the economics of the physical commodity of book, while the third overlaps the spheres of both. All these difficulties should be examined and removed.